Volume 1

BUILDER'S ADVANTAGE: Home Plans ™

Henry O. Evans

Copyright 2017

Builder's Advantage: Home Plans Volume 1

Henry O. Evans Design Collection, LLC.

All Rights Reserved. No part of this publication may be reproduced, stored in a retrieval system, or transmitted, in any form or by any means, electronic, mechanical photocopying, recording, or otherwise without prior written permission of the publisher. The information in this book is true and complete to the best of our knowledge. All recommendations are made without guarantee on the part of the author or Henry O. Evans Design Collection, LLC. The author and publisher disclaim any liability with the use of this information. For additional information please contact Henry O. Evans Design Collection, LLC. at P.O. Box 85, Springfield Mo. 65801.

Henry O. Evans Design Collection, LLC. published books are available for special premium and promotional uses for customized editions. For further information, please call 1-888-356-8085.

The Builder's Advantage: Home Plans Volume 1, is an easy to use guide for selecting home planning services, showcasing the most popular and bestselling home plans offered by Henry O. Evans Design Collection, LLC. from the Henry O. Evans Design Collection, LLC. Library. It includes, English/Spanish Useful Expressions, English/Spanish Glossary, and Glossary covering Residential Contracting, Real Estate and Project Management terms. This volume is assembled within four categories of residential design styles such as, Brick & Stone, Mediterranean, Mountain Home & Cabin, and Coastal.

We hope that with use of the Builders' Advantage: Home Plans Volume 1, you are able to find our plans pleasing to buyers in your market. Also, learn about the Science of Project Management, Building Information Modeling (BIM), Factoring Costs, tips for Effective Land Usage, and Going GREEN.

All home designs within this publication have been designed by Henry O. Evans, and are copyright registered with the U.S. Library of Congress. Our effort is to make great residential home design available to builders of all sizes, from small to large. Within this collection, we bring pristinely innovative architecturally designed housing to builders, developers and individuals at an affordable price.

Contents

Pg. 29

Pg. 13

Pg. 53

Pg. 39

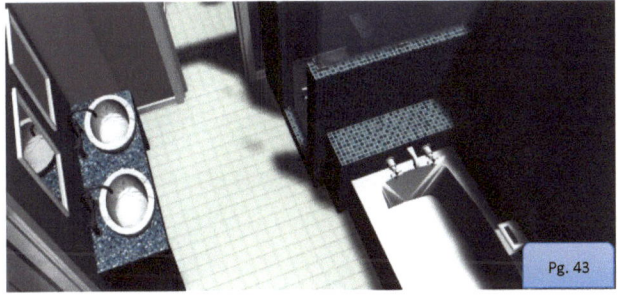

Pg. 43

Articles & Information

Publisher's Corner	2
About Us and Our Services	3
The Science of Project Management	14
Benefits of Building Information Modeling (BIM)	24
Going GREEN?	44
Factoring the Cost: Cost Estimating Tips	54
10 Reason's to Choose Narrow Lot Home Plans	60
Copyright Laws	34
Glossary	68
English / Spanish Glossary	78
English / Spanish Useful Expressions	82

Home Designs

Copper Penny	6
Centurion	10
Archie Bunker	16
Blue Sails	20
Bellevedeiri	26
Atascacita	30
Cambria	36
Breezy Palacade	40
Honey Stone	46
Israelite	50
Autumn Leaf	56
Cocoa Cabana	62

How to Order

What is in a Set?	4
How to Use This Plan Book?	5
Change and Modification Process?	66
Resources & References	67

Builder's Advantage: Home Plans Volume 1

TO ORDER CALL: 1-888-356-8085 *or* henryevansdesign.com

Henry O. Evans
Founder and Editorial Director

Legal Notice

All notices from Henry O. Evans Design Collection, LLC to You may be posted on our Web site and will be deemed delivered within thirty (30) days after posting. Notices from You to Henry O. Evans Design Collection, LLC shall be made either by regular mail, sent to the address we provide on our Web site, or first-class mail to our address at: P.O. Box 85, Springfield, Mo. 65801

Delivery shall be deemed to have been made by You to Henry O. Evans Design Collection, LLC five (5) days after the date sent.

Copyright Notice

All content appearing within this publication is the property of:

Henry O. Evans Design Collection, LLC.

Copyright © 2017 Henry O. Evans Design Collection, LLC. All rights reserved. As a user, you are authorized only to view, copy, print, and distribute documents on this publication so long as (1) the document is used for informational purposes only, and (2) any copy of the document (or portion thereof) includes the following copyright notice: Copyright © 2017 Henry O. Evans Design Collection, LLC. All rights reserved.

Trademarks

All brand, product, service, and process names appearing on this publication are trademarks of their respective holders. Reference to or use of a product, service, or process does not imply recommendation, approval, affiliation, or sponsorship of that product, service, or process by Henry O. Evans Design Collection, LLC. Nothing contained herein shall be construed as conferring by implication, estoppel, or otherwise any license or right under any patent, copyright, trademark, or other intellectual property right of Henry O. Evans Design Collection, LLC or any third party, except as expressly granted herein.

Terms of Use

This publication may contain other proprietary notices and copyright information, the terms of which must be observed and followed. Information on this site may contain technical inaccuracies or typographical errors. Information, including product pricing and availability, may be changed or updated without notice. Henry O. Evans Design Collection, LLC and its subsidiaries reserve the right to refuse service, terminate accounts, and/or cancel orders in its discretion, including, without limitation, if Henry O. Evans Design Collection, LLC believes that customer conduct violates applicable law or is harmful to the interests of Henry O. Evans Design Collection, LLC and its subsidiaries.

Privacy Policy

This publication may contain other proprietary notices and copyright information, the terms of which must be observed and followed. Information on this site may contain technical inaccuracies or typographical errors. Information, including product pricing and availability, may be changed or updated without notice. Henry O. Evans Design Collection, LLC and its subsidiaries reserve the right to refuse service, terminate accounts, and/or cancel orders in its discretion, including, without limitation, if Henry O. Evans Design Collection, LLC believes that customer conduct violates applicable law or is harmful to the interests of Henry O. Evans Design Collection, LLC and its subsidiaries.

Shipping and Delivery

At this time, Henry O. Evans Design Collection, LLC ships merchandise to locations within the United States and U.S. territories, including Alaska, Hawaii, Puerto Rico, Guam, and the US Virgin Islands. Additionally, Henry O. Evans Design Collection, LLC ships merchandise to Canada and Mexico, but not to other international locations. The risk of loss and title for all merchandise ordered through this publication and on Web site pass to you when the merchandise is delivered to the shipping carrier.

International

Customs and import duties may be applied to International orders when the shipment reaches its destination. Such charges are the responsibility of the recipient of your order and vary from country to country. Contact your local customs office for details.

Shipping laws are different in each country. It is your responsibility to check with your Customs office to verify whether the country to which you are shipping permits the shipment of your products. Henry O. Evans Design Collection, LLC is not responsible for any direct, indirect, punitive, or consequential damages that arise from improper international shipping practices.

Welcome to *Builder's Advantage* and thank you for considering us for your new home building plans. *Builder's Advantage* is a Henry O. Evans Design Collection, LLC. Publication that is dedicated to creating quality home plans, while incorporating innovative techniques, to modernize the building design and construction process.

These beautiful home designs are crafted using the Science of Project Management and the power of Building Information Modeling, which is a revolutionary building design and construction technology. As you read, view the luxurious; Brick & Stone, Mediterranean, Mountain Home & Cabin, and Coastal styled design of the homes as well as the energy saving, eco-friendly options that we offer.

It's our hope that you're satisfied with Henry O. Evans Design Collection, *Builder's Advantage: Home Plans Volume 1*. Enjoy this plan book and thank you again.

Cecil McBrayer, Jr.

**Cecil McBrayer, Jr.
Editor In Chief**

TO ORDER CALL: 1-888-356-8085 *or* henryevansdesign.com

HENRY O. EVANS DESIGN COLLECTION, LLC.

ABOUT US

Our founder, Henry O. Evans holds a BSc. In Project Management and Administration – Construction. We have eighteen plus years of experience designing residential home plans and creating construction documents. We have worked with several home builders and industry professionals within the United States. Because of our background in Project Management and Administration - Construction, we are able to Initiate, Plan, Organize, Staff, Guide, Monitor and Control Construction Projects through an integrated process to meet identified requirements on time and budget. Also, we are equipped with a variety of techniques to help manage, coordinate, and supervise the construction process from concept development through project completion on a timely and economic basis.

With this unique combination of Residential Home Design and Construction Documentation with Project Management Tools & Techniques we are able to help our clients add ease and efficiency to the overall construction process. This aides positively while working with builders, developers, and individual home owners alike wherein we are able to stream-line the building design and construction process.

We are also members of the following organizations: American Institute of Building Design (AIBD), Construction Specifications Institute (CSI), Design Build Institute of America (DBIA), and Project Management Institute (PMI).

OUR SERVICES

Our Areas of Specialization: Custom Home Design, Stock Home Plans, Concept Development / Animation, Construction Project Scheduling, Project Management Tools & Techniques, Construction Cost Estimating, Management of Global Projects, Procurement and Contract Management, Building Codes, Construction Techniques, Project Risk Management, Project Quality Management, Project Cost and Budget Management, and Project Communication and Documentation.

Builder's Advantage: Home Plans Volume 1   TO ORDER CALL: 1-888-356-8085   *or*   henryevansdesign.com

What is in a set?

A Construction Document Set.

Each Plan Set Includes Components Such as Floor Plans, Dimensions, Cross Sections, and Elevations That Specify How Your House is to Be Built. Individual Plan Packages May Include:

1. COVER SHEET, Showcases an artists rendering of the outside of the finished house. Lists sheet index, project and dwelling summary, as well as other pertinent project data.

2. SPECIFICATIONS SHEET, contain all aspects of a specification and lists all materials to be used in building or renovating a structure.

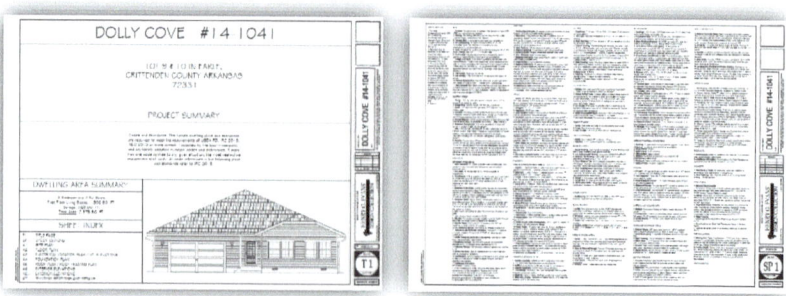

3. FOUNDATION PLAN, Includes layout of foundation, support walls, plus excavated and unexcavated areas, if applicable.

4. DETAILED FLOOR PLANS, Show the layout of each floor of the house, including room dimensions, window and door sizes, and keys for cross section details provided later in the plans. The location of kitchen appliances, bathroom fixtures and location for electrical fixtures, switches and outlets that may also be specified. Electrical locations may be shown on separate sheet for clarity.

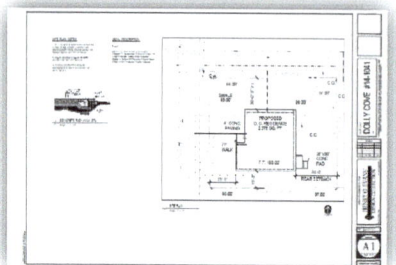 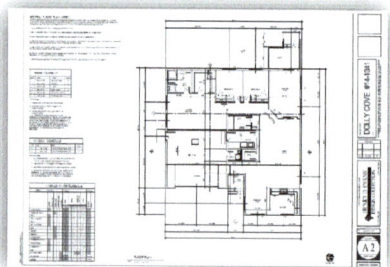

5. INTERIOR ELEVATIONS, These drawings show the specific details and design of cabinets, fireplaces, bookcases and other special interior features.

6. FLOOR FRAMING PLANS, Show complete layout and necessary details for ceiling and floor framing. Include joist location, size and direction of components, stair openings, and floor heights. When trussses are used, it is recommended to use a local truss manufaturer, to ensure compliance with local codes and regulations.

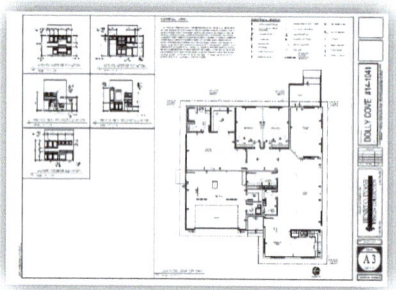 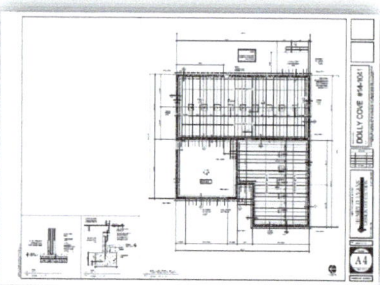

7. ROOF PLAN, Includes the overall layout and necessary details for the construction of the roof. When trussses are used, it is recommended to use a local truss manufaturer, to ensure compliance with local codes and regulations.

8. EXTERIOR ELEVATIONS, Views of front, rear, left, and right side of the exterior of the house are included. Also, noted are materials of the exterior construction, details, and measurements.

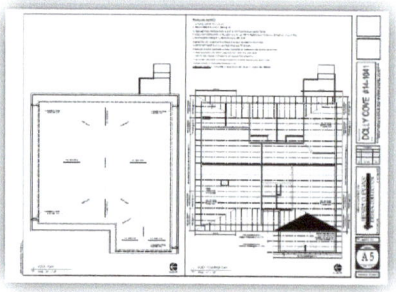 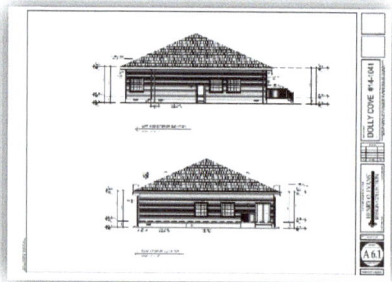

9. CROSS SECTIONS and BUILDING DETAILS, Show important relationship from one level to another are called out in when there are changes in floor, ceiling and roof heights.

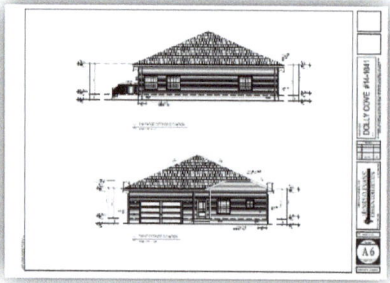 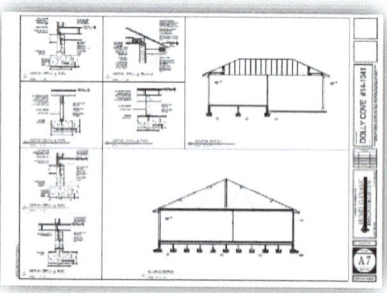

TO ORDER CALL: **1-888-356-8085** *or* henryevansdesign.com

Builder's Advantage: Home Plans Volume 1

How to Use This Plan Book

CALCULATION of SQUARE FOOTAGES

Square footage calculations are taken from the construction of the exterior walls outside face and include all interior walls windows and room projections of air-conditioned space. Areas that are not included, are un-air-conditioned space such as porches, decks, attics, garages, and carports.

Note: Because mechanical - plumbing codes and their design considerations differ widely across the country, mechanical and plumbing drawings are not included. This percentage of the home design is usually left to the contractor to determine. Our home plans include sufficient details for construction requirements; to provide information for permitting, contracting and construction in the municipality where the project will be built. Our construction documents graphically convey the appropriate design requirements for a construction project and adjusted to meet the requirements of local building departments, as well as local, state and national laws statues and building codes that may be applicable.

PURCHASING OF PRINTS

You may purchase complete sets of construction documents in PDF, Vellum, or CAD format.:

1. PDF's are available in right reading or 'mirror image' that in reverse image not including the lettering.
2. Vellum's are available to be printed as often as required. Builder may use as original tracing to make alterations to suit a specific client, individual construction method, material selection, or local code requirements.
3. CAD files are electronic versions of drawings and can also be printed as often as required for necessary alterations by builder.

ORDER FORM

To charge on MasterCard or Visa, call Toll free 1-888-356-8085 or send check to:

Henry O. Evans Design Collection, LLC.
P.O. Box 85, Springfield, Mo. 65801

Name_____
Company Name_____
Address_____
City/State/Zip_____
Credit Card number_____
Expiration number_____
Telephone number_____
Signature_____

HOW MANY SETS DO YOU NEED?

___ **OWNER**, Usually requires (2) sets; (1) set for notes and (1) set for file.

___ **BUILDER**, Usually requests (5) sets; (1) as a legal document, (1) for inspections and at least (3) to give subcontractors.

___ **LOCAL BUILDING DEPARTMENT**, Often only requires (3) sets.

___ **MORTGAGE LENDER**, Usually requires (4) sets; (1) set for a conventional loan and (3) sets for FHA or Va loans.

___ **TOTAL NUMBER OF SETS NEEDED**

BUILDER'S ADVANTAGE: Home Plans ™

*Our value package offering included with purchase of any home plan design.

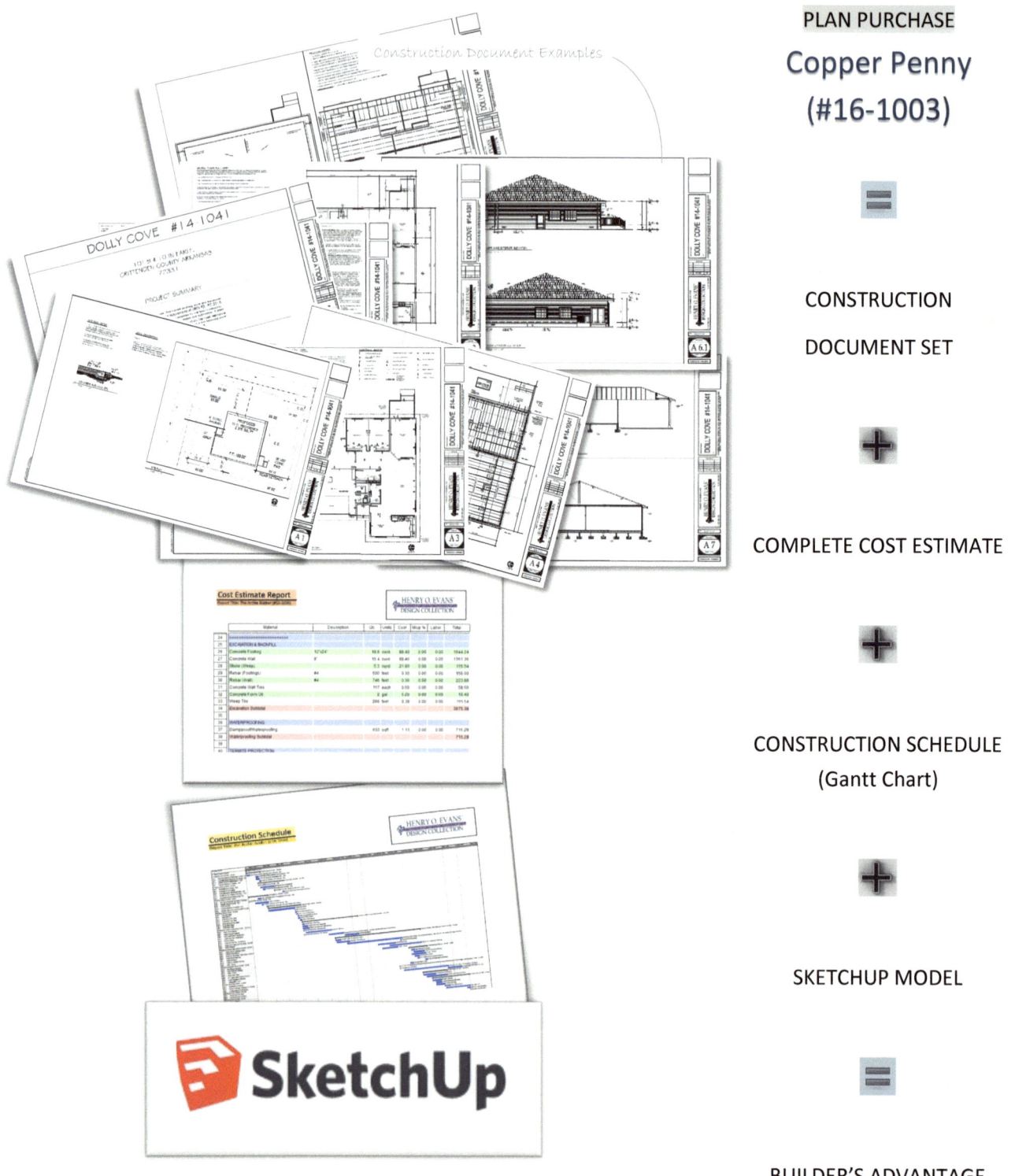

PLAN PURCHASE

Copper Penny (#16-1003)

=

CONSTRUCTION DOCUMENT SET

+

COMPLETE COST ESTIMATE

+

CONSTRUCTION SCHEDULE (Gantt Chart)

+

SKETCHUP MODEL

=

BUILDER'S ADVANTAGE (Value Package)

TO ORDER CALL: 1-888-356-8085 or henryevansdesign.com

Builder's Advantage: Home Plans Volume 1

"The Copper Penny - HOEDC-16-1003" © 2017 Henry O. Evans Design Collection, LLC.

Copper Penny

PLAN NUMBER: HOEDC-16-1003

BEDROOMS: 3

BATHS: 3 ½

WIDTH: 31'-0"

DEPTH: 51'-0"

1ST FLOOR: 849 sq. ft.

2ND FLOOR: 1187 sq. ft.

LIVING AREA: 2036 sq. ft.

FOUNDATION: Crawl Space

PRICES

1 SET: $740

5 SETS: $862

8 SETS: $937

VELLUM or PDF: $1073

CAD: $1864

Welcome Home! This lovely Brick & Stone styled home design, welcomes you in a friendly, yet stunning manner. Romantic elements of its design, ascend to a modern blend of contemporary rustic and indigenous influences.

Builder's Advantage: Home Plans Volume 1   **TO ORDER CALL: 1-888-356-8085** *or* henryevansdesign.com

Summer 2017 | Pg.7

Designed to capture spectacular sunset views, the covered decks mingle harmoniously with wood columns and brackets and allow all design elements to flow generously. Gracefully sculpted forms, punctuated by splendid aesthetics, combine to create casual beauty and quiet elegance. Adobe brick walls, quoins, and accented bands add texture that embraces the formation of this homes picturesque exterior. While sited within a place of breath taking beauty, its compatibility mixes deeply with elegant surroundings.

First Floor

Second Floor

Luxe Design Features:

- Beautiful covered – cozy decks, suitable through all seasons (spring, summer, fall, and winter).
- A captivating and exciting entry, with attractive curb appeal that eases the senses.
- Full kitchen, powder bath, master bath spacious living area, exquisite master bedroom, and cozy lounge area.

PLAN NAME: **Copper Penny** PLAN NUMBER: HOEDC-16-1003 PRICING: 1 SET: $740, 5 SETS: $862, 8 SETS: $937, VELLUM or PDF: $1073, CAD: $1864

TO ORDER CALL: 1-888-356-8085 or henryevansdesign.com   Builder's Advantage: Home Plans Volume 1

© "THE COPPER PENNY, HOEDC-16-1003" (2017), HENRY O. EVANS DESIGN COLLECTION, LLC.

PLAN NAME: Copper Penny **PLAN NUMBER:** HOEDC-16-1003 **PRICING:** 1 SET: $740, 5 SETS: $862, 8 SETS: $937, VELLUM or PDF: $1073, CAD: $1864

Builder's Advantage: Home Plans Volume 1   **TO ORDER CALL: 1-888-356-8085** *or* **henryevansdesign.com**

BUILDER'S ADVANTAGE: Home Plans ™

*Our value package offering included with purchase of any home plan design.

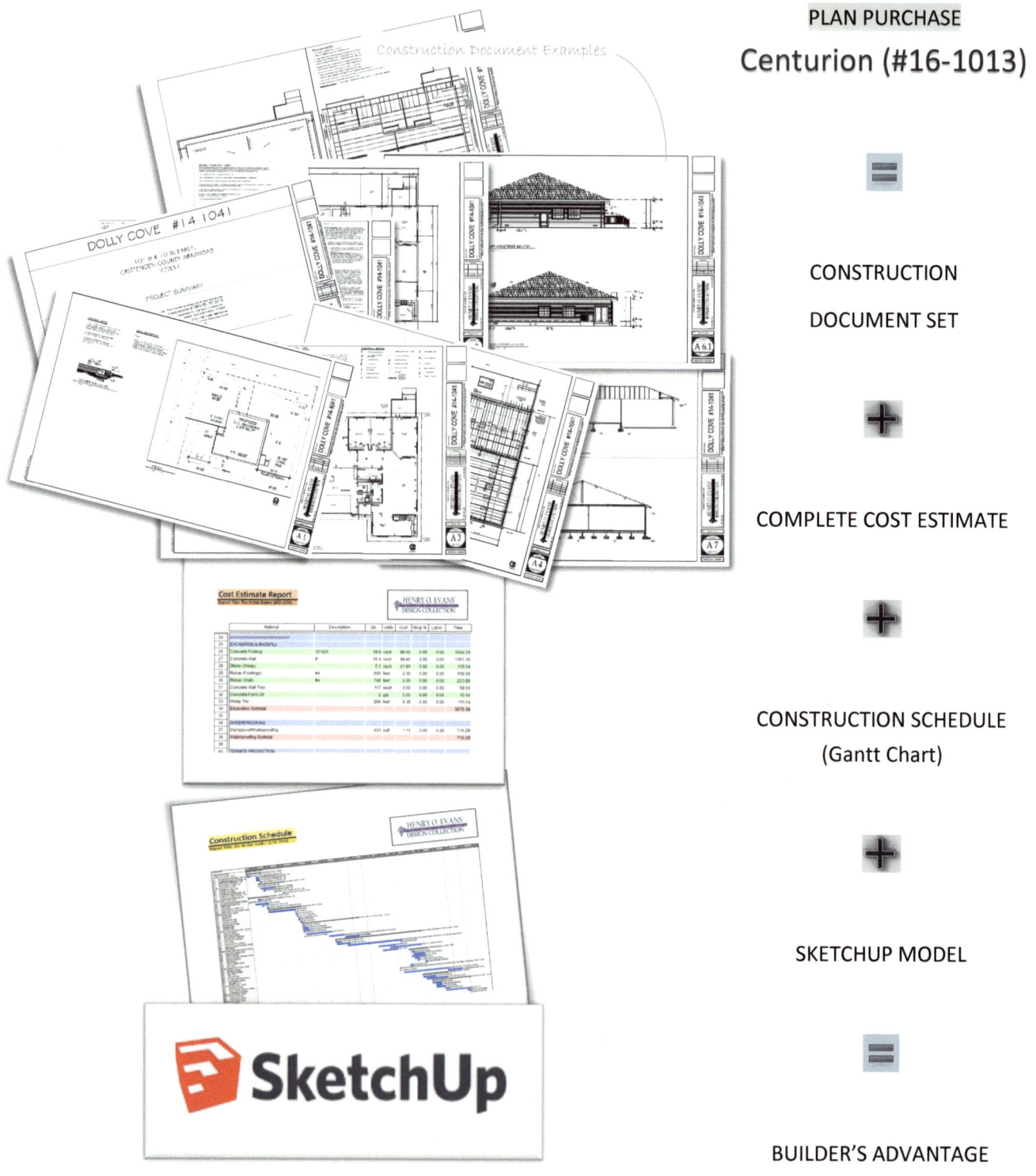

PLAN PURCHASE

Centurion (#16-1013)

=

CONSTRUCTION DOCUMENT SET

+

COMPLETE COST ESTIMATE

+

CONSTRUCTION SCHEDULE
(Gantt Chart)

+

SKETCHUP MODEL

=

BUILDER'S ADVANTAGE
(Value Package)

TO ORDER CALL: 1-888-356-8085 or henryevansdesign.com

Builder's Advantage: Home Plans Volume 1

"The Centurion - HOEDC-16-1013" © 2017 Henry O. Evans Design Collection, LLC.

Centurion

PLAN NUMBER: HOEDC-16-1013

BEDROOMS: 3

BATHS: 3 ½

WIDTH: 31'-0"

DEPTH: 51'-0"

1ST FLOOR: 914 sq. ft.

2ND FLOOR: 1294 sq. ft.

LIVING AREA: 2208 sq. ft.

FOUNDATION: Crawl Space

PRICES

1 SET: $740

5 SETS: $862

8 SETS: $937

VELLUM or PDF: $1073

CAD: $1864

Customized Luxury That Integrates a Variety of Mediterranean Styled Elements Eclectic to Past Splendor And True To New-Age Technology.

Builder's Advantage: Home Plans Volume 1

TO ORDER CALL: 1-888-356-8085 or henryevansdesign.com

A country feel of rustic splendor tempers a gentle mix of past and present. It's gracefully crafted facade is carefully designed to fit a splendor lot in which is not only cozy, it is also, comfortable and magnificently nestled into a beautiful home design. This home plans beautiful entry foyer and curved walls present a cozy transition through-out the family room, kitchen-dining area and up to the master suite.

First Floor

Second Floor

Luxe Design Features:

- Romantic exterior railing, rustic wood accents, and decorative stone blend beautifully with its classic red clay tiled roof.
- Beautiful entry foyer adds excitement and ease within a grouping of several other magnificent surroundings.
- An open flow between the kitchen and seating area allows two modest size spaces to function as one large gathering area.

PLAN NAME: **Centurion**   PLAN NUMBER: HOEDC-16-1013   PRICING: 1 SET: $740, 5 SETS: $862, 8 SETS: $937, VELLUM or PDF: $1073, CAD: $1864

TO ORDER CALL: 1-800-746-9953   or   henryevansdesign.com   Builder's Advantage: Home Plans Volume 1

© "THE CENTURION, HOEDC-16-1013" (2017), HENRY O. EVANS DESIGN COLLECTION, LLC.

PLAN NAME: **Centurion** PLAN NUMBER: HOEDC-16-1013 PRICING: 1 SET: $740, 5 SETS: $862, 8 SETS: $937, VELLUM or PDF: $1073, CAD: $1864

Builder's Advantage: Home Plans Volume 1   TO ORDER CALL: 1-888-356-8085 *or* henryevansdesign.com

Summer 2017 | Pg.13

Now more than ever, more and more professionals are acknowledging the need and usefulness of project management.

The Science of PROJECT MANAGEMENT

By H. Evans

Everything is a project. Everywhere you look in our society today, project management has risen to cover many assorted operational systems for several diversified organizations and yet its general principles remain central to its core operational structure.

Our construction cost estimates list all materials in quantified and itemized allocation. Each construction cost estimate is specific to each home plan selected. Although other systems utilize a one size fits all approach, we remain consistent within the scope definition of each home plan individually.

TO ORDER CALL: 1-888-356-8085 *or* henryevansdesign.com

Builder's Advantage: Home Plans Volume 1

Now more than ever, more and more people are acknowledging the need and usefulness of project management. Many are starting to notice the effectiveness that cross-references systems within the managerial formats through several different organizations. Although it's related processes can be equally applied to several diverse structures, many technical skills are still required to be coupled in hand with an expansive array of personable skills when executed. As described by Jeffrey K. Pinto in his writings within, *Project Management: Achieving the Competitive Advantage*; he says, "We live in a projectized world". By this expression, I realize that everything is a project in one form or the other (Pinto 2010).

Everything is a project. Everywhere you look in our society today, project management has risen to cover many assorted operational systems for several diversified organizations and yet its general principles remain central to its core operational structure. What all projects have in common, is that they are all established to formulate a distinctive product, result, or service. Simply speaking, all projects are distinctive in relation to other similar projects, even with the same models and systems. For example, many homes can be constructed using the same materials and plans, however different locations make each project uniquely different because of the locations stakeholders, specific conditions, climate circumstances, and local situations (PMBOK 2013).

Our home plans are packaged to include helpful technical aspects such as a construction cost estimate and a construction schedule in the form of a Gantt chart, because this will help create ease and efficiency during the overall construction process. Our construction cost estimates list all materials in quantified and itemized allocation. Each construction cost estimate is specific to each home plan selected. Although other systems utilize a one size fits all approach, we remain consistent within the scope definition of each home plan individually. Our construction schedules allocate task, resources, and milestones to assist in the process of completing construction projects on-time and on-budget.

Builder's Advantage: Home Plans Volume 1   TO ORDER CALL: 1-888-356-8085 *or* henryevansdesign.com

BUILDER'S ADVANTAGE: Home Plans ™

*Our value package offering included with purchase of any home plan design.

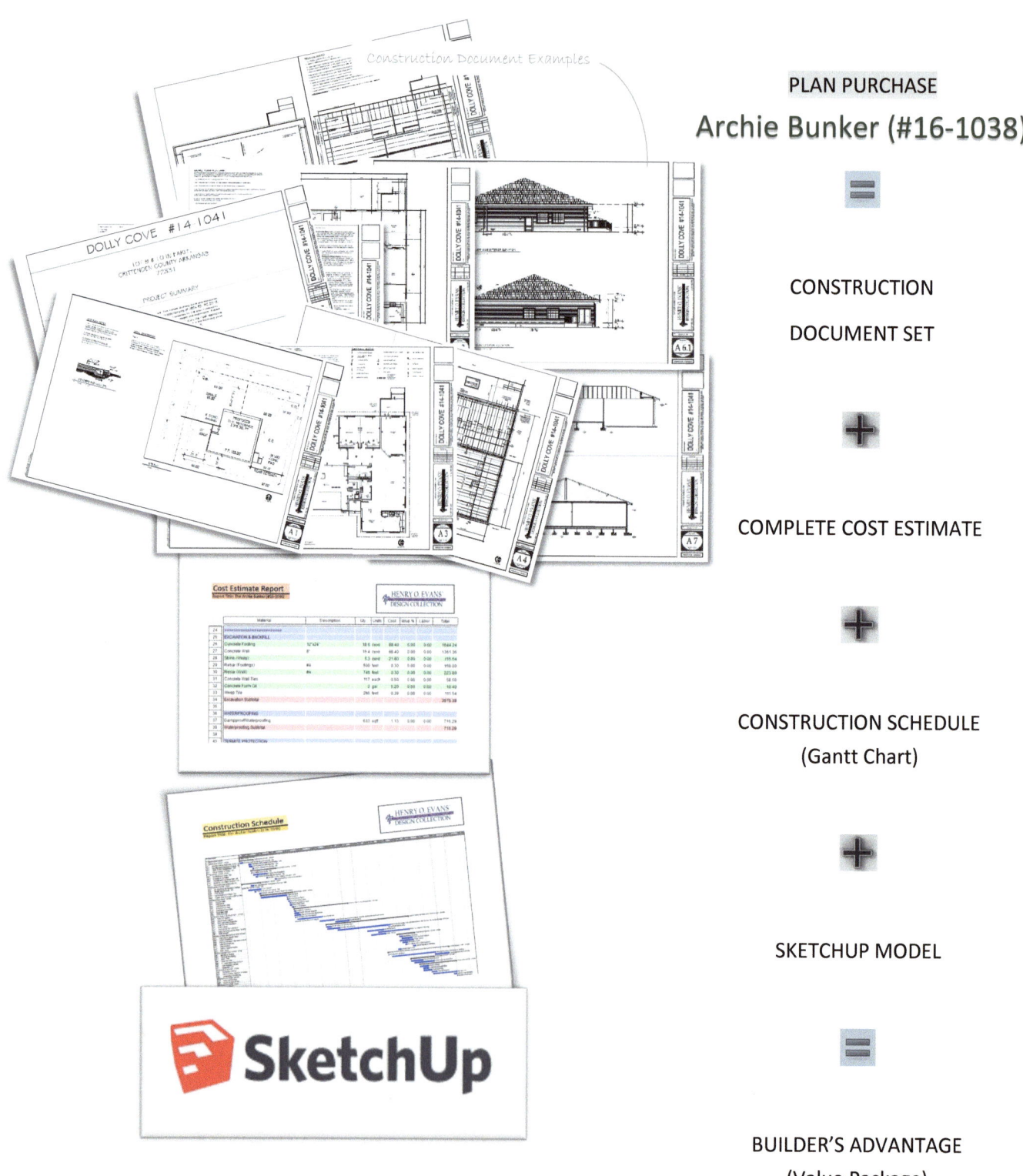

PLAN PURCHASE
Archie Bunker (#16-1038)

=

CONSTRUCTION DOCUMENT SET

+

COMPLETE COST ESTIMATE

+

CONSTRUCTION SCHEDULE
(Gantt Chart)

+

SKETCHUP MODEL

=

BUILDER'S ADVANTAGE
(Value Package)

TO ORDER CALL: 1-888-356-8085 *or* henryevansdesign.com

"The Archie Bunker - HOEDC-16-1038" © 2017 Henry O. Evans Design Collection, LLC.

First Floor

Second Floor

Archie Bunker

PLAN NUMBER: HOEDC-16-1038

BEDROOMS: 3

BATHS: 3 ½

WIDTH: 31'-0"

DEPTH: 51'-0"

1ST FLOOR: 760 sq. ft.

2nd FLOOR: 1209 sq. ft.

LIVING AREA: 1969 sq. ft.

FOUNDATION: Crawl Space

PRICES

1 SET: $740

5 SETS: $862

8 SETS: $937

VELLUM or PDF: $1073

This craftsman sensation avowals a wonderful series of gables, that add vigor to its Mountain Home & Cabin styled design. Beauty and charm of the exterior emits a friendly and welcoming feel generating peaceful tranquility that easily sets hardness at ease.

Builder's Advantage: Home Plans Volume 1

TO ORDER CALL: 1-888-356-8085   or   henryevansdesign.com

A wonderful combination of siding embellishes the exterior of this attractive design. An impressive covered porch opens to a wonderful open deck and features elegant French doors that permit an easy transition throughout each space. Outdoor entertaining is a breeze in this home, with several outdoor spaces to commune and entertain.

First Floor

Second Floor

Luxe Design Features:

- Wood and stone siding mixes elegantly with the garage and roof color-tones.
- Its beautiful kitchen is both classic and high-tech, to support key areas aiding in ease during food preparation.
- Cozy lounge area, Graceful master bath, and practical master bedroom arrangement allows functionality and comfort to collide peacefully.

PLAN NAME: **Archie Bunker** PLAN NUMBER: HOEDC-16-1038 PRICING: 1 SET: $740, 5 SETS: $862, 8 SETS: $937, VELLUM or PDF: $1073, CAD: $1864

TO ORDER CALL: 1-888-356-8085 *or* henryevansdesign.com

Builder's Advantage: Home Plans Volume 1

© "THE ARCHIE BUNKER, HOEDC-16-1003" (2017), HENRY O. EVANS DESIGN COLLECTION, LLC.

PLAN NAME: Archie Bunker PLAN NUMBER: HOEDC-16-1038 PRICING: 1 SET: $740, 5 SETS: $862, 8 SETS: $937, VELLUM or PDF: $1073, CAD: $1864

Builder's Advantage: Home Plans Volume 1   TO ORDER CALL: 1-888-356-8085   *or*   henryevansdesign.com

BUILDER'S ADVANTAGE: Home Plans ™

*Our value package offering included with purchase of any home plan design.

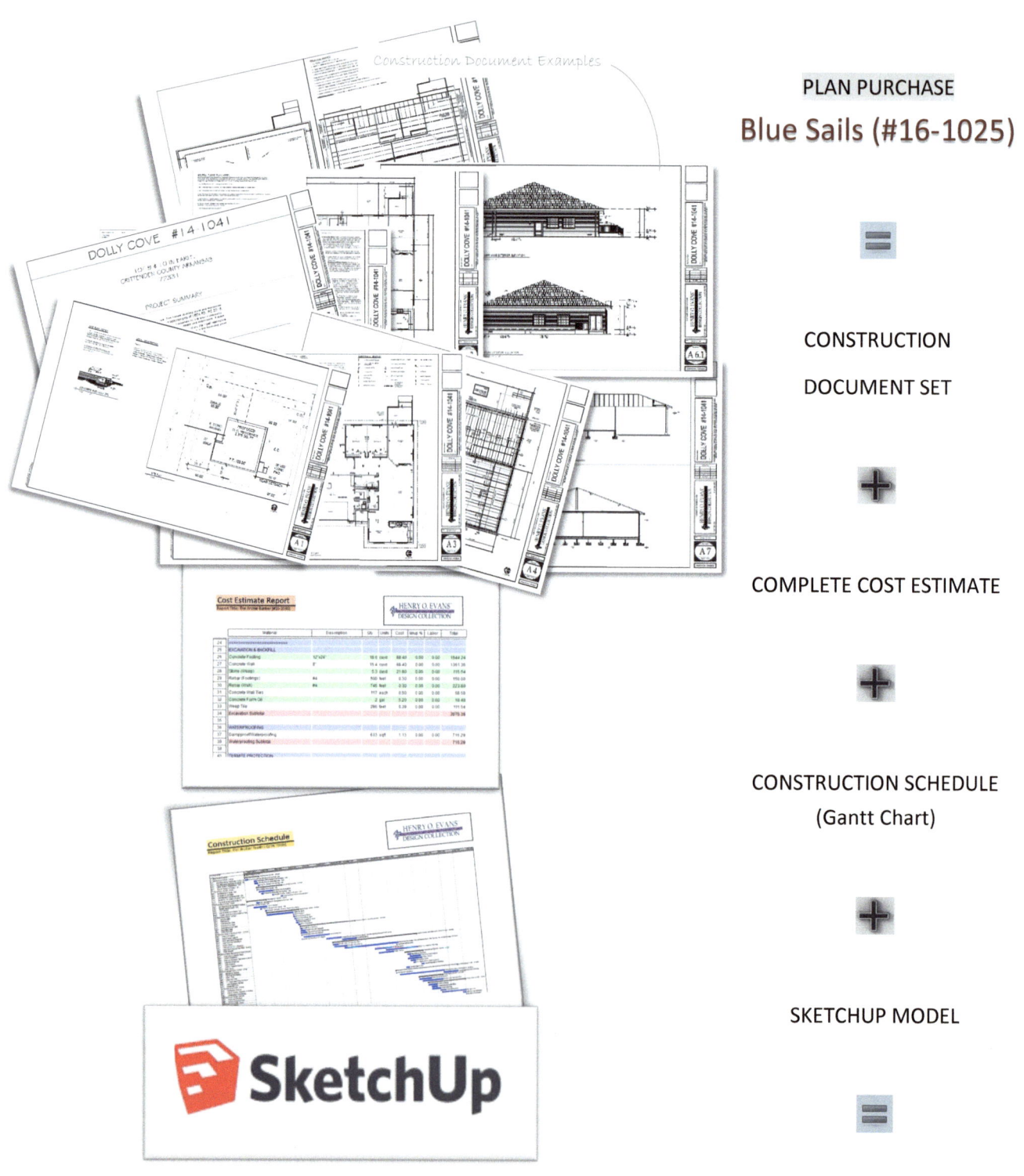

PLAN PURCHASE

Blue Sails (#16-1025)

=

CONSTRUCTION DOCUMENT SET

+

COMPLETE COST ESTIMATE

+

CONSTRUCTION SCHEDULE
(Gantt Chart)

+

SKETCHUP MODEL

=

BUILDER'S ADVANTAGE
(Value Package)

TO ORDER CALL: 1-888-356-8085 or henryevansdesign.com

"The Blue Sails - HOEDC-16-1025" © 2017 Henry O. Evans Design Collection, LLC.

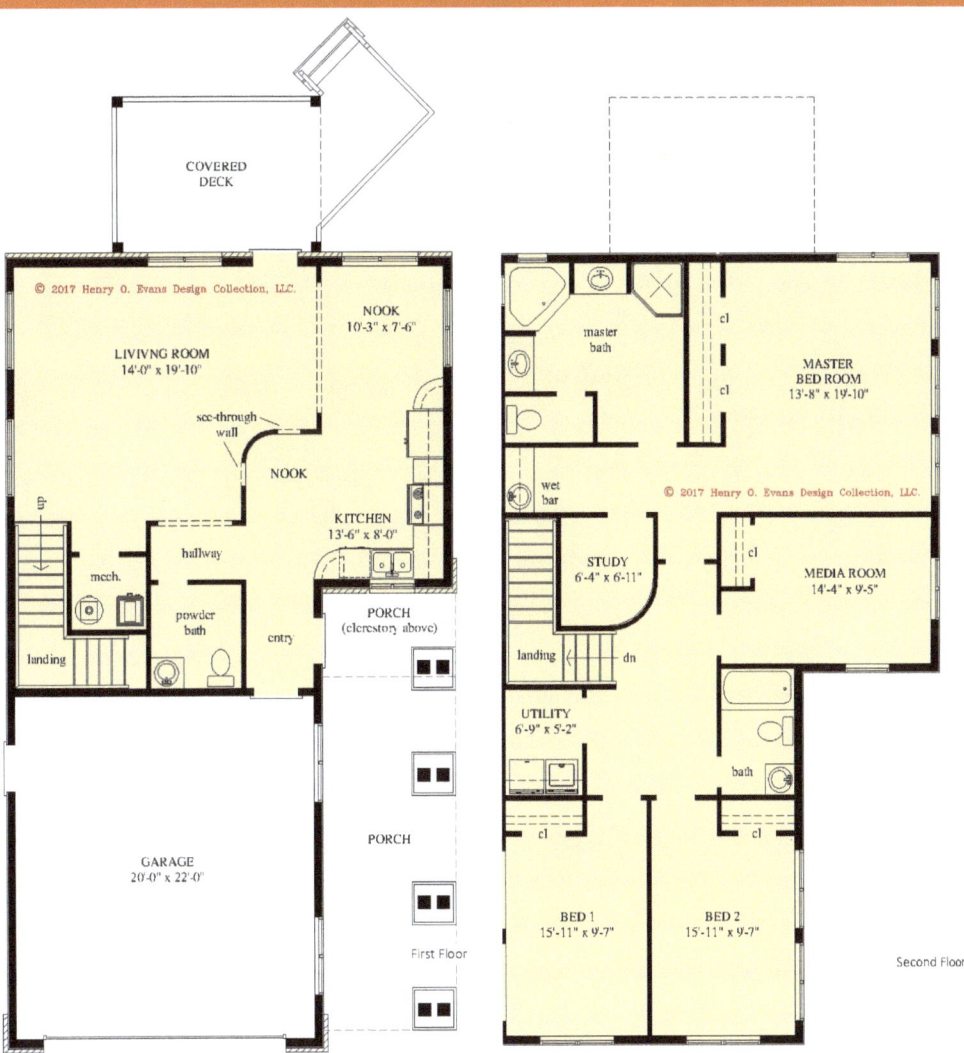

Blue Sails

PLAN NUMBER: HOEDC-16-1025

BEDROOMS: 3

BATHS: 2 ½

WIDTH: 31'-0"

DEPTH: 51'-0"

1ST FLOOR: 789 sq. ft.

2ND FLOOR: 1299 sq. ft.

LIVING AREA: 2088 sq. ft.

FOUNDATION: Crawl Space

PRICES

1 SET: $740

5 SETS: $862

8 SETS: $937

VELLUM or PDF: $1073

CAD: $1864

This Coastal styled design, celebrates new craftsman inspiration and flare. Its bold specialty windows and stone accents assimilate a stylish and unique shape, while mansard roofs unite to create a striking appearance.

Builder's Advantage: Home Plans Volume 1   TO ORDER CALL: 1-888-356-8085 or henryevansdesign.com

Classic siding enhances the covered porch, achieving a balanced allocation of basics by optimizing features of traditional craftsman panache and modern coastal elements. An enchanting entry-way boasts a wonderful series of double columns, which invite beauty and depth to venture within. Designed to celebrate waterfront surroundings, its well-appointed windows capture breath taking views of the sea, lake, or pond.

Luxe Design Features:

- The exterior emits a friendly and welcoming feel. A beautifully positioned covered porch entry sets the stage for the spacious glow and warmth of the interior.
- This waterfront design aptly addresses a seaboard patois and is well suited for beach dwellers and vacationing owners.
- Its high energy frontage oxygenates the curb appeal with beachy aesthetics that emphasize the waterfront location.

PLAN NAME: Blue Sails PLAN NUMBER: HOEDC-16-1025 PRICING: 1 SET: $740, 5 SETS: $862, 8 SETS: $937, VELLUM or PDF: $1073, CAD: $1864

TO ORDER CALL: 1-888-356-8085 *or* henryevansdesign.com   Builder's Advantage: Home Plans Volume 1

© "THE BLUE SAILS, HOEDC-16-1025" (2017), HENRY O. EVANS DESIGN COLLECTION, LLC.

PLAN NAME: Blue Sails **PLAN NUMBER:** HOEDC-16-1025 **PRICING:** 1 SET: $740, 5 SETS: $862, 8 SETS: $937, VELLUM or PDF: $1073, CAD: $1864

Builder's Advantage: Home Plans Volume 1

TO ORDER CALL: 1-888-356-8085 *or* henryevansdesign.com

Summer 2017 | Pg.23

Benefits of BIM!?

BIM is an acronym for Building Information Modeling (BIM). Building Information Modeling (BIM) is object-based modeling in the platform of building design and construction documentation. *By H. Evans*

BIM models are specific to their domain, meaning they can carry information of each specific object and the overall building itself, and therefore considered to be "smart". Traditional computer-aided design (CAD) is primarily 2D and generally describe data within the platform of building design and construction documentation using lines, points, planes, and rectangles. For many designers who have used CAD know that it has been a ground-breaking advancement for several years, however CAD is somewhat limited because it doesn't carry information about the building itself within its geometric entities (AGS 2013). BIM allows changes and modifications to be done quickly and efficiently. BIM overcomes this limitation within CAD and allows changes and modifications to be transferred throughout all of its design media simultaneously. This is not a new concept and has been in development since the 1970's, however the majority of companies using design have recently gravitated to these applications since 2010.

TO ORDER CALL: 1-888-356-8085 or henryevansdesign.com   Builder's Advantage: Home Plans Volume 1

Another benefit that can be utilized with BIM is the opportunity to extract much needed information from the model, for the purpose of analysis, design, and construction management. Many problems associated with CAD and manual drafting, can now be overcame by the use of a BIM applications (AGS 2013).

Although we utilize the application of BIM systems, we are still able to efficiently merge and work with the traditional standards of CAD.

Our Home Plans utilize BIM within several aspects of the design process. Because design conflicts can be easily detected within the buildings model, BIM is considered cost effective. This makes it more efficient and time-consuming, nonetheless highly reducing expensive adjustments during construction. BIM data within the modeled objects can be extracted and used simultaneously with construction specifications and cost related expenditures. Because the models carry information of each object and the building, each object has the specified material and can be directly linked to the specifications format. Also, all modeled materials can easily show quantity's and cost related expenditures, allowing quantity takeoffs to be easily imported into applications such as RS Means data (Mubarak 2012).

Builder's Advantage: Home Plans Volume 1   TO ORDER CALL: 1-888-356-8085 *or* henryevansdesign.com

BUILDER'S ADVANTAGE: Home Plans ™

*Our value package offering included with purchase of any home plan design.

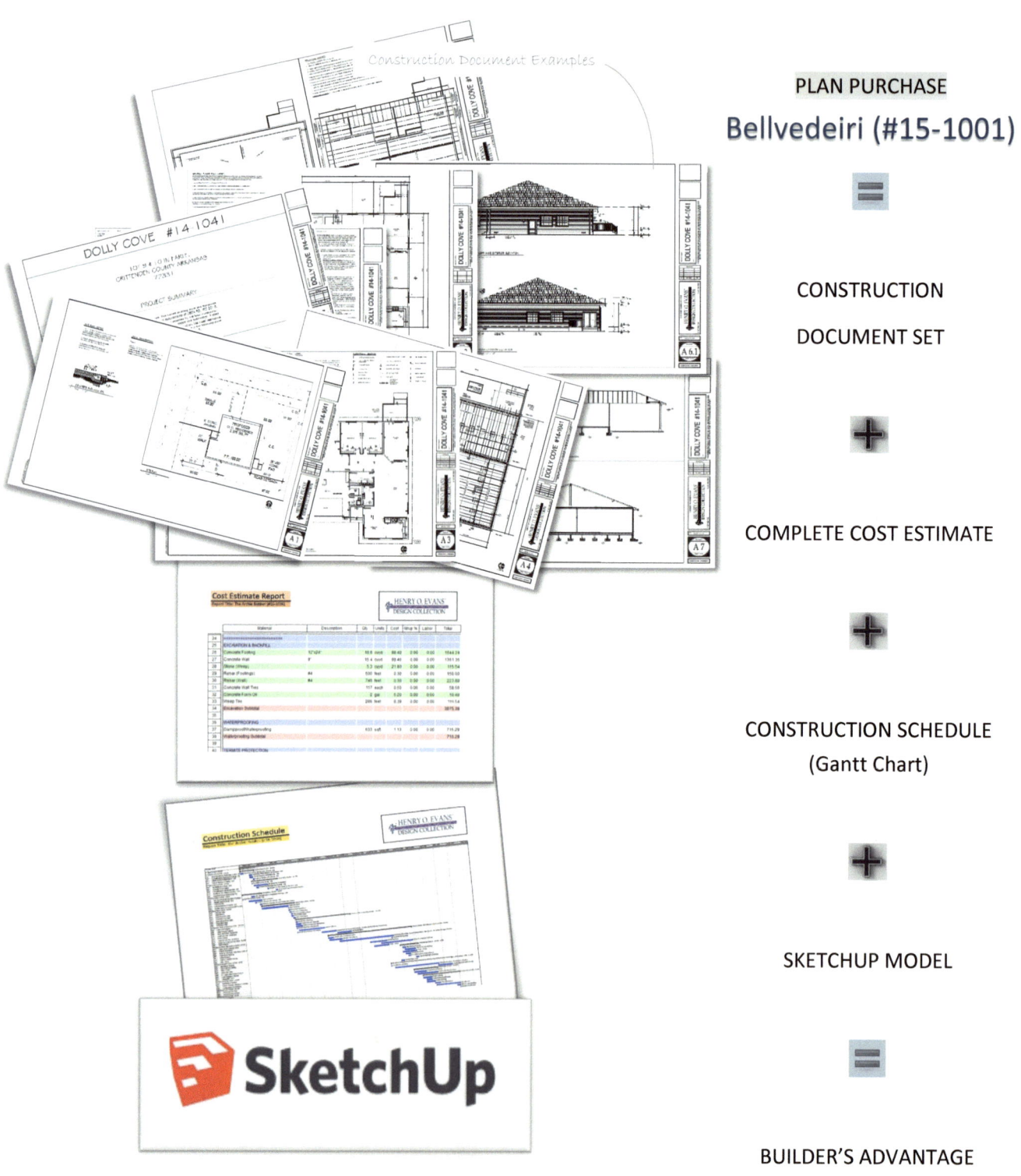

PLAN PURCHASE

Bellvedeiri (#15-1001)

=

CONSTRUCTION

DOCUMENT SET

+

COMPLETE COST ESTIMATE

+

CONSTRUCTION SCHEDULE

(Gantt Chart)

+

SKETCHUP MODEL

=

BUILDER'S ADVANTAGE

(Value Package)

TO ORDER CALL: 1-888-356-8085 or henryevansdesign.com

Builder's Advantage: Home Plans Volume 1

"The Bellvedeiri - HOEDC-15-1001" © 2017 Henry O. Evans Design Collection, LLC.

First Floor

Second Floor

Bellvedeiri

PLAN NUMBER: HOEDC-15-1001

BEDROOMS: 3

BATHS: 2 ½

WIDTH: 31'-0"

DEPTH: 51'-0"

1ST FLOOR: 739 sq. ft.

2ND FLOOR: 1351 sq. ft.

LIVING AREA: 2098 sq. ft.

FOUNDATION: Crawl Space

PRICES

1 SET: $740

5 SETS: $862

8 SETS: $937

VELLUM or PDF: $1073

CAD: $1864

This brick home is overflowing with casually elegant details. Its artistic nook and sitting rooms provide a positioning for multiple views, while spiral columns, diamond, and stone accents enhance the setting of this beautiful combination.

Builder's Advantage: Home Plans Volume 1   TO ORDER CALL: 1-888-356-8085   or   henryevansdesign.com

Romantic elements of its Brick and Stone styled design ascend to a modern blend of contemporary modern mixed features. Designed to capture spectacular sunset views the exterior window placement mingles harmoniously with a properly transitioned interior, that is full of free-form and functionality.

First Floor

Second Floor

Luxe Design Features:

- Beautiful curb appeal blends effortlessly with the comfortable kitchen and romantically refreshing master bath.
- Efficient flow of the interior kitchen layout, offers function and step-saving for multiple cooks while family gathering.
- Double walk-in closets transition into the cozy master bath retreat.

PLAN NAME: **Bellvedeiri** PLAN NUMBER: HOEDC-15-1001 PRICING: 1 SET: $740, 5 SETS: $862, 8 SETS: $937, VELLUM or PDF: $1073, CAD: $1864

TO ORDER CALL: 1-888-356-8085 or henryevansdesign.com   Builder's Advantage: Home Plans Volume 1

PLAN NAME: **Bellvedeiri** PLAN NUMBER: HOEDC-15-1001 PRICING: 1 SET: $740, 5 SETS: $862, 8 SETS: $937, VELLUM or PDF: $1073, CAD: $1864

Builder's Advantage: Home Plans Volume 1   TO ORDER CALL: 1-888-356-8085   or   *henryevansdesign.com*

BUILDER'S ADVANTAGE: Home Plans ™

*Our value package offering included with purchase of any home plan design.

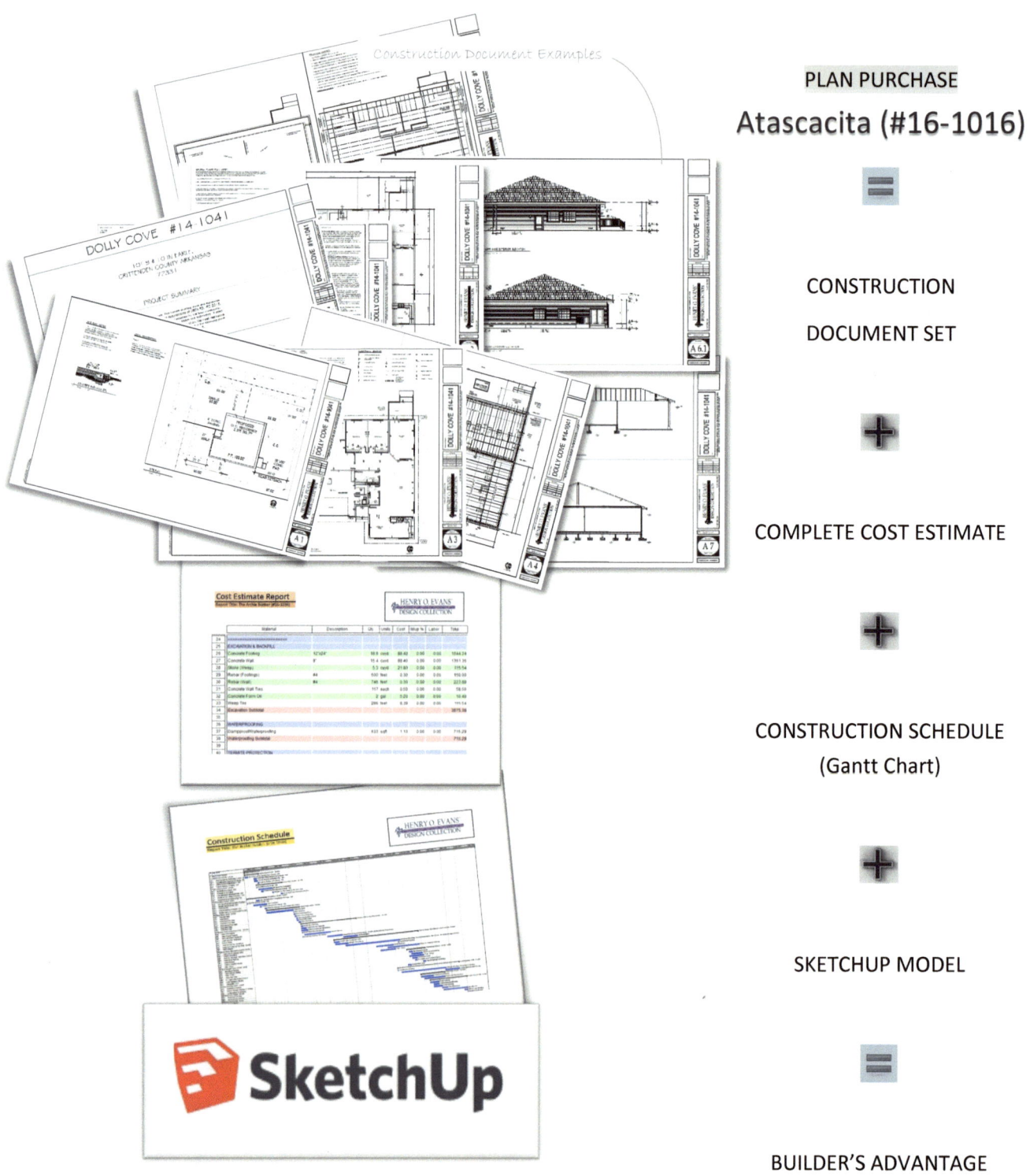

PLAN PURCHASE

Atascacita (#16-1016)

=

CONSTRUCTION

DOCUMENT SET

+

COMPLETE COST ESTIMATE

+

CONSTRUCTION SCHEDULE

(Gantt Chart)

+

SKETCHUP MODEL

=

BUILDER'S ADVANTAGE

(Value Package)

TO ORDER CALL: 1-888-356-8085   or   henryevansdesign.com

"The Atascacita - HOEDC-16-1016" © 2017 Henry O. Evans Design Collection, LLC.

Atascacita

PLAN NUMBER: HOEDC-16-1016

BEDROOMS: 3

BATHS: 2 ½

WIDTH: 31'-0"

DEPTH: 51'-0"

1ST FLOOR: 886 sq. ft.

2ND FLOOR: 1203 sq. ft.

LIVING AREA: 2089 sq. ft.

FOUNDATION: Crawl Space

PRICES

1 SET: $740

5 SETS: $862

8 SETS: $937

VELLUM or PDF: $1073

CAD: $1864

Encircling the elegance of a unique Mediterranean styled retreat, this stylish home design mixes high-tech luxury with traditional ingenuity. A pristinely innovative exterior adorned with a creative blend of fittings embellish the ornamental facade of this lovely home.

Builder's Advantage: Home Plans Volume 1

TO ORDER CALL: 1-888-356-8085 *or* henryevansdesign.com

Integrating a variety of stylish elements, the exterior is unified using a uniquely positioned courtyard combined with traditional iron work, brackets aligned with corbels, and colorful clay tiled roofs. Like a watch tower, the front decks of this attractive home design enhance the serene landscape and sets the tone for luxurious spaces within.

First Floor

Second Floor

Luxe Design Features:

- A unique curved entry creates exuberance before entering the great room of this attractive home.
- This crisp kitchen design rejoices enthusiastically with daring solid color tones, while the island support seating is key placement for providing ease when preparing food.
- Creative and comfortable bedroom placement offer pristinely innovative space allotments for a modern and high-tech palate.

PLAN NAME: **Atascacita** PLAN NUMBER: HOEDC-16-1016 PRICING: 1 SET: $740, 5 SETS: $862, 8 SETS: $937, VELLUM or PDF: $1073, CAD: $1864

TO ORDER CALL: 1-888-356-8085 *or* henryevansdesign.com   Builder's Advantage: Home Plans Volume 1

© "THE ATASCACITA, HOEDC-16-1016" (2017), HENRY O. EVANS DESIGN COLLECTION, LLC.

PLAN NAME: Atascacita   PLAN NUMBER: HOEDC-16-1016   PRICING: 1 SET: $740, 5 SETS: $862, 8 SETS: $937, VELLUM or PDF: $1073, CAD: $1864

Builder's Advantage: Home Plans Volume 1   TO ORDER CALL: 1-888-356-8085   *or*   henryevansdesign.com

Summer 2017 | Pg.33

COPYRIGHT LAWS

The United States copyright law protects "original works of authorship," fixed in a tangible medium including literary, dramatic, musical, artistic, and other intellectual works. This protection is available to both published and unpublished works.

WHAT YOU SHOULD KNOW ABOUT COPYRIGHTS

All plans sold through our publications are protected by The United States Copyright Act. Reproduction of these plans, either in whole or in part, including any form of copying, distribution, dissemination, preparation, of derivative works therefrom, for any reason without prior written permission, is strictly prohibited. The purchase of a set of home plans in no way transfers any copyright or other ownership interest in it to the buyer except for a limited license to use that set of home plans for the construction of a dwelling unit.

Similarly, the purchase of reproducible home plans (vellums, sepias, mylars) carries the same copyright protection as stated above. Whereas a purchaser of the reproducible plan is granted a license to make copies for the purchaser's use in the construction of dwelling units, making photocopies from our bond drawings is illegal.

Copyright and licensing of home plans for construction exists to protect all parties. It respects and supports the intellectual property of the original home designer or publisher.

Willful infringement could cause settlements for statutory damages up to $150,000 plus attorney fees, damages and loss of profits.

HOME PLANS ARE COPYRIGHTED

Just like books, movies, and songs, federal copyright law protects the intellectual property of architects and home designers by giving copyright protection to home plans and designs. These legal protections exist to protect all parties. The copyright law prevents anyone from reproducing, modifying or reusing the plans or design without written permission from the copyright owner.

WHO IS RESPONSIBLE FOR COPYRIGHT INFRINGEMENT?

Any party who participates in copyright violation may be responsible, including the purchaser, designers, architects, engineers, drafters, homeowners, builders, contractors, subcontractors, printers, developers and real estate agencies. It does not matter whether the individual knows that a violation is being committed. Remember: ignorance of the law is not a valid defense. Refuse to be a party to any illegal copying or use of designs, derivative works, prints or design features by being certain of the original plan source.

DON'T COPY DESIGNS OR FLOOR PLANS FROM ANY PUBLICATION

It is illegal to create construction drawings from home designs found in any plan book, CD-ROM or on the internet. It is a common misunderstanding that it is permissible to copy, adapt or change a floor plan or design found in any media. It is not. It is also illegal to copy a constructed home that is protected by copyright, even if you have never seen the plan for the home. If a particular home plan or existing home is desired, a set of plans must be purchased from an authorized source.

REPRODUCIBLE HOME PLANS

Reproducible plans come with a license to copy, as well as to make modifications to the plans, for the purchaser's own use. Once modified, the plans can be taken to a printer to make copies. This license does not include the right to sell or distribute copies to others.

TO ORDER CALL: 1-800-746-9953 *or* henryevansdesign.com   Builder's Advantage: Home Plans Volume 1

COPYRIGHT LAWS

PLANS AND BLUEPRINTS CANNOT BE COPIED OR REPRODUCED

Plans and blueprints cannot be copied. If additional sets are required, please contact us to purchase additional sets (within thirty (30) days of original purchase) at a nominal cost. Printers are prohibited from making copies of these plans.

DON'T REDRAW BLUEPRINTS WITHOUT PERMISSION

Plans may not be redrawn or modified without first obtaining the copyright owner's written permission. With your purchase of plans, you are permitted to make non-structural changes by "red-lining" the purchased plans. "Redlined" plans are still copyrighted and cannot be copied. If you need to make major changes or need to have the plans redrawn for any reason you may contact our office for modification services.

MODIFIED DESIGNS CANNOT BE REUSED

Even if you are licensed to make modifications to a copyrighted design, the modified design is not free from the original designer's copyright. This is considered derivative work. The sale or reuse of the modified design is prohibited. Also, be aware that any modification to the plan relieves the designer from liability for design defects and voids all warranties expressed or implied.

PLEASE RESPECT THE DESIGNERS COPYRIGHTS

In the event of a suspected violation of a copyright, or if there is any uncertainty about the plans purchased, the publisher, designer or Council of Publishing Home Designers should be contacted before proceeding. Rewards are sometimes offered for information about the home design copyright infringement.

PENALTIES FOR INFRINGEMENT

Penalties for violating copyright may be severe. The responsible parties are required to pay actual damages caused by the infringement (which may be substantial), plus any profits made by the infringer. The copyright law also allows for recovery of statutory damages, which may be as high as $150,000 for each infringement. Finally, the infringer may be required to pay legal fees, which often exceed the damages.

COPY RIGHT LAW of the **UNITED STATES** and Related Laws contained in Title 17 of the United States Code
https://www.copyright.gov/title17/

BUILDER'S ADVANTAGE: Home Plans ™

*Our value package offering included with purchase of any home plan design.

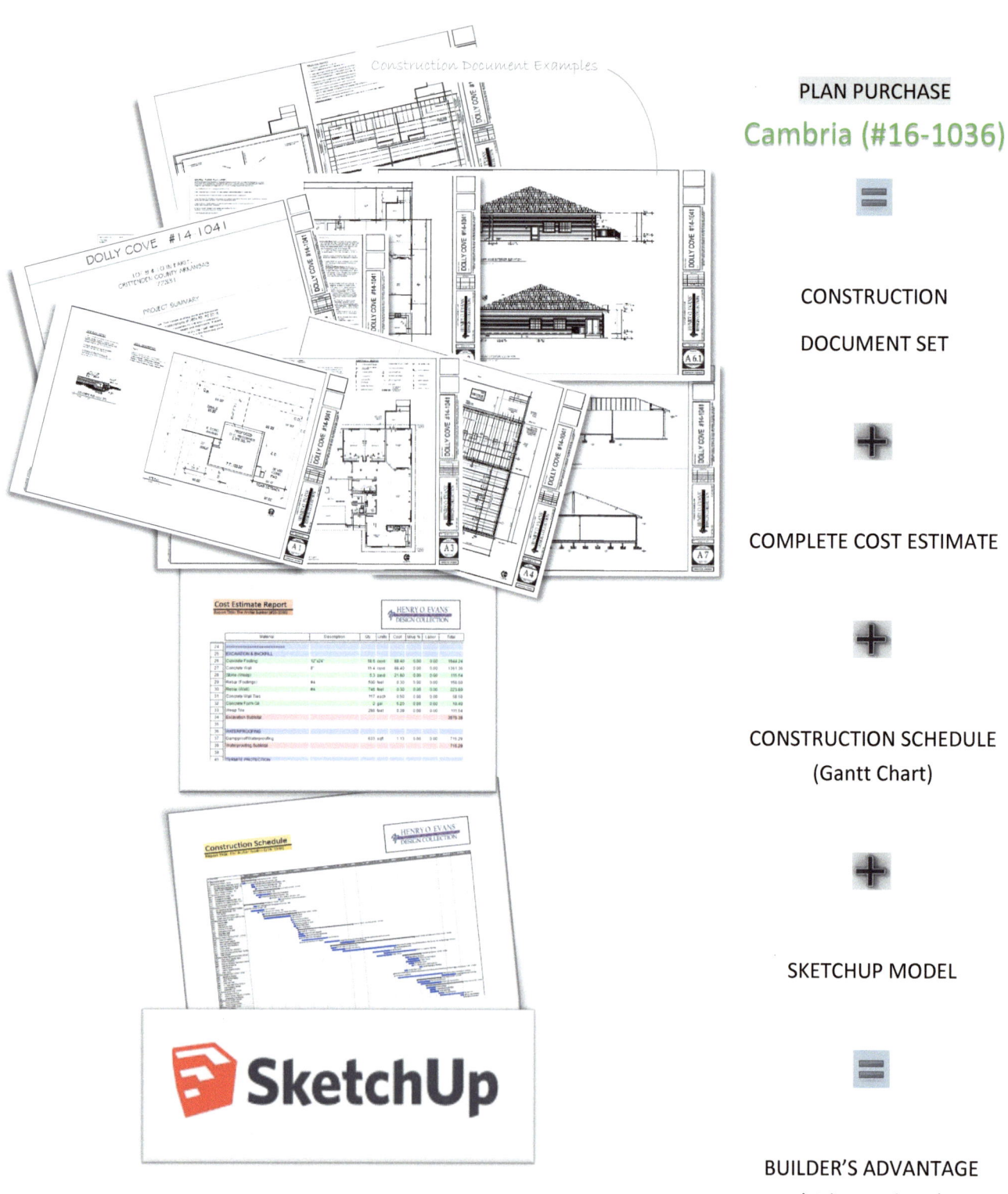

PLAN PURCHASE

Cambria (#16-1036)

=

CONSTRUCTION DOCUMENT SET

+

COMPLETE COST ESTIMATE

+

CONSTRUCTION SCHEDULE
(Gantt Chart)

+

SKETCHUP MODEL

=

BUILDER'S ADVANTAGE
(Value Package)

TO ORDER CALL: 1-888-356-8085 or henryevansdesign.com

Builder's Advantage: Home Plans Volume 1

"The Cambria - HOEDC-16-1036" © 2017 Henry O. Evans Design Collection, LLC.

Cambria

PLAN NUMBER: HOEDC-16-1036

BEDROOMS: 3

BATHS: 3 ½

WIDTH: 31'-0"

DEPTH: 51'-0"

1ST FLOOR: 858 sq. ft.

2ND FLOOR: 1263 sq. ft.

LIVING AREA: 2121 sq. ft.

FOUNDATION: Crawl Space

PRICES

1 SET: $740

5 SETS: $862

8 SETS: $937

VELLUM or PDF: $1073

CAD: $1864

A tranquil and serene feel is radiated when you see its pretty exterior. Sensationally crafty and quietly elegant, this Mountain Home & Cabin styled design, also vaunts a series of gables with wood accents and angled openings. Its specialty windows are signature to its style and allow outdoor viewing a must.

Builder's Advantage: Home Plans Volume 1   TO ORDER CALL: 1-888-356-8085 or henryevansdesign.com

Distinctive with warm texture and dimension, its unique garage roof is accented with brackets and topped off with a wonderful combination of cedar shake and stone siding. This charming exterior makes way for the spacious interior rich with elegant moldings and crafted panels. Make it yours to live in year-round or as a get-away once a year, likewise way you'll always come home for vacation!

First Floor

Second Floor

Luxe Design Features:

- A careful sequence of rooms permits the design to proceed freely and function properly throughout each space.
- Peaceful aesthetics, creating a harmonious curb appeal and peaceful scenery.
- Spacious rooms, full functional and equipped with all the amenities. Its kitchen layout is designed to last changing family needs and equipped to accommodate several users.

PLAN NAME: **Cambria**   PLAN NUMBER: HOEDC-16-1036   PRICING: 1 SET: $740, 5 SETS: $862, 8 SETS: $937, VELLUM or PDF: $1073, CAD: $1864

TO ORDER CALL: 1-888-356-8085   *or*   henryevansdesign.com

Builder's Advantage: Home Plans Volume 1

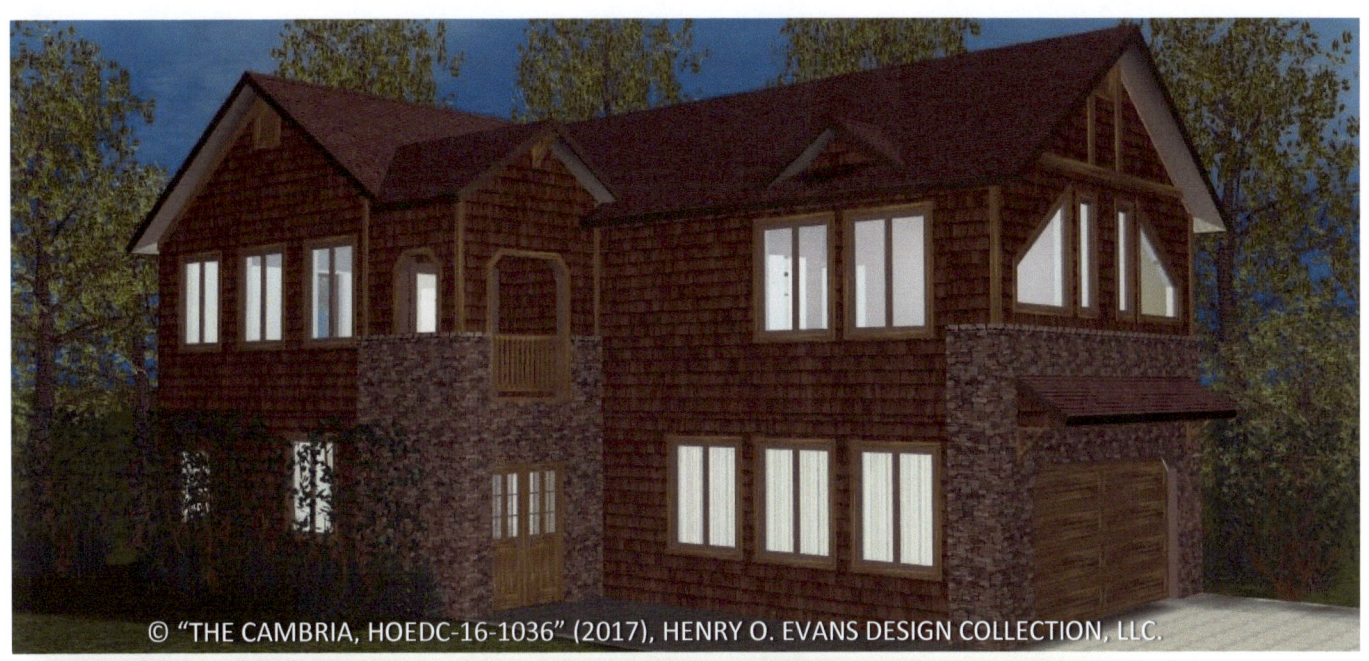

© "THE CAMBRIA, HOEDC-16-1036" (2017), HENRY O. EVANS DESIGN COLLECTION, LLC.

PLAN NAME: Cambria **PLAN NUMBER:** HOEDC-16-1036 **PRICING:** 1 SET: $740, 5 SETS: $862, 8 SETS: $937, VELLUM or PDF: $1073, CAD: $1864

Builder's Advantage: Home Plans Volume 1   TO ORDER CALL: 1-888-356-8085 *or* henryevansdesign.com

BUILDER'S ADVANTAGE: Home Plans ™

*Our value package offering included with purchase of any home plan design.

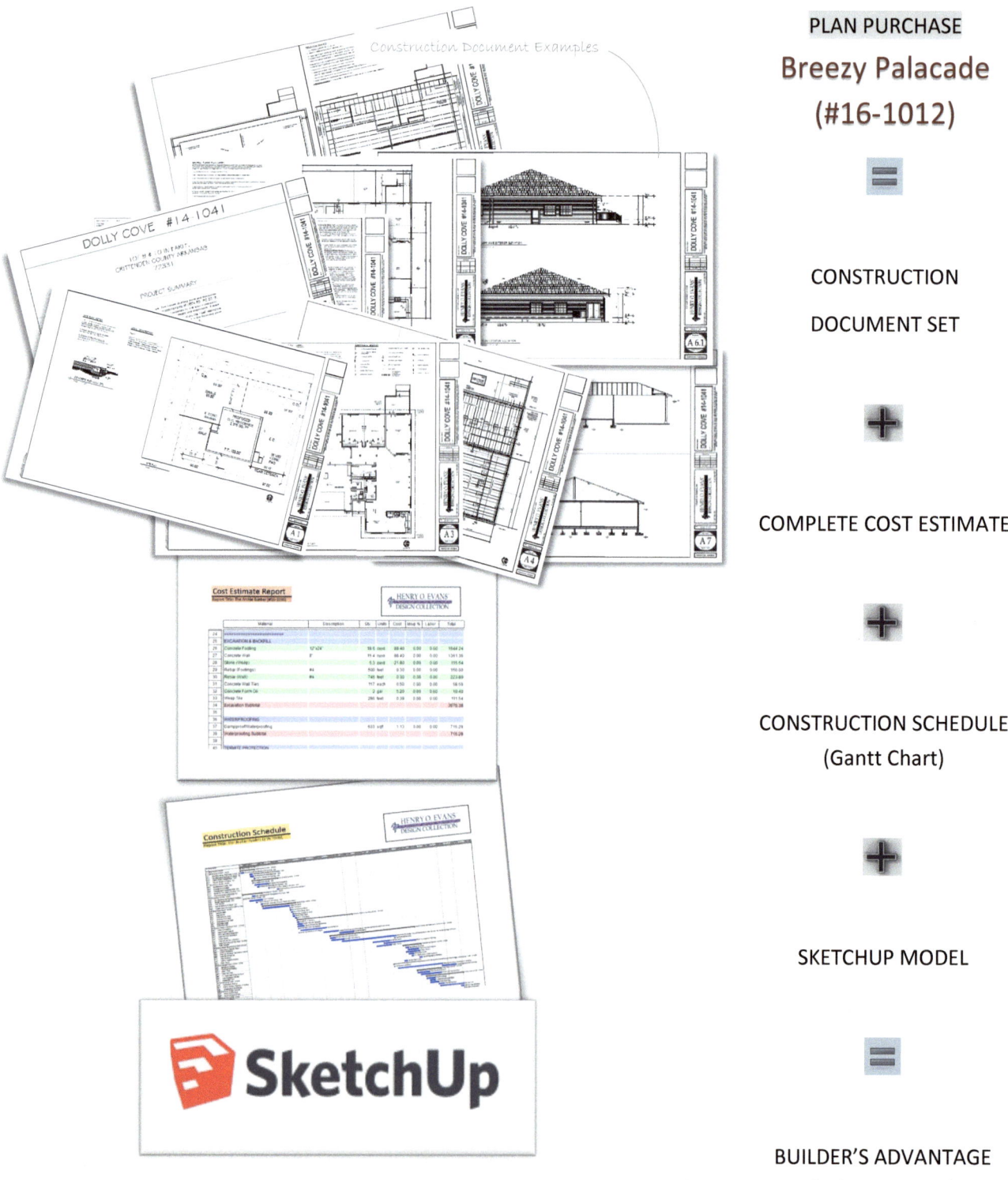

PLAN PURCHASE

Breezy Palacade (#16-1012)

=

CONSTRUCTION DOCUMENT SET

+

COMPLETE COST ESTIMATE

+

CONSTRUCTION SCHEDULE
(Gantt Chart)

+

SKETCHUP MODEL

=

BUILDER'S ADVANTAGE
(Value Package)

TO ORDER CALL: 1-888-356-8085 *or* henryevansdesign.com

Builder's Advantage: Home Plans Volume 1

"The Breezy Palacade - HOEDC-16-1012" © 2017 Henry O. Evans Design Collection, LLC.

Breezy Palacade

PLAN NUMBER: HOEDC-16-1012

BEDROOMS: 3

BATHS: 3 ½

WIDTH: 31'-0"

DEPTH: 51'-0"

1ST FLOOR: 799 sq. ft.

2ND FLOOR: 1247 sq. ft.

LIVING AREA: 2046 sq. ft.

FOUNDATION: Crawl Space

PRICES

1 SET:	$740
5 SETS:	$862
8 SETS:	$937
VELLUM or PDF:	$1073
CAD:	$1864

Crisp modern elements contribute usefully to the luxury of this homes exterior impression, while a tropical aesthetics add flare and ambience to its Mediterranean styled design. Radiant luxury is attainable, if you dream of living an exquisite lifestyle within this stunning home.

First Floor

Second Floor

Builder's Advantage: Home Plans Volume 1   TO ORDER CALL: 1-888-356-8085   or   henryevansdesign.com

Its summer inspired exterior features an open arrangement of forms that facilitate a graceful tour of sun, sand, and sea. This homes design mixes wide open views with various functional details. Cozy covered porches feature French doors and a colonnade of arched openings that allow the inner and outside spaces to flow harmoniously.

First Floor

Second Floor

Luxe Design Features:

- A mixture of historic charm and striking forms promote a relaxed lavish hide-a-way.
- Its coastal flare invigorates a waterfront lifestyle, while the breezy covered decks seem suitable for any warm climate.
- Full functional kitchen, beautifully refreshing master bath, and curved walls are cutting edge for new homes within this exciting new modern era.

PLAN NAME: **Breezy Palacade**   PLAN NUMBER: HOEDC-16-1012   PRICING: 1 SET: $740, 5 SETS: $862, 8 SETS: $937, VELLUM or PDF: $1073, CAD: $1864

TO ORDER CALL: 1-888-356-8085 or henryevansdesign.com   Builder's Advantage: Home Plans Volume 1

Summer 2017 | Pg.42

© "THE BREEZY PALACADE, HOEDC-16-1012" (2017), HENRY O. EVANS DESIGN COLLECTION, LLC.

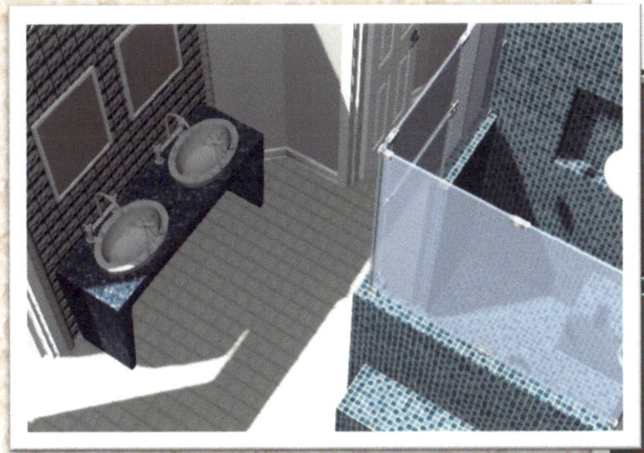

PLAN NAME: Breezy Palacade **PLAN NUMBER:** HOEDC-16-1012 **PRICING:** 1 SET: $740, 5 SETS: $862, 8 SETS: $937, VELLUM or PDF: $1073, CAD: $1864

Builder's Advantage: Home Plans Volume 1

TO ORDER CALL: 1-888-356-8085 *or* henryevansdesign.com

Air Polution

Going GREEN?

Remarkable Energy Saving Materials can reduce pollutants from product emissions. *By H. Evans*

Going green is a term coined to describe the process of using environmentally safe building products and materials. Within green and/or environmentally friendly building design and construction, energy efficiency is assessed. To accomplish this in buildings, the design documents must select materials that are energy efficient and environmentally friendly. This can seam simple at a first look; however certain cautions should be taken when approaching these selections. For example, just because many materials are considered green and/or environmentally friendly, doesn't mean that they don't have a high fire rating. For this reason, we believe, all selections must be cross-referenced with the building code requirements, first and foremost. Going green, is assessing Energy Efficiency in Building Structures and Design. The major driver for energy efficiency compliance in residential and commercial building construction is mostly based from, the cost of energy, building performance, and government regulations. Many owners move toward energy efficiency or green building because of the price of energy for new and existing facilities. Easy aspects to measure, emanate from occupant well-being, satisfaction, and savings.

TO ORDER CALL: 1-888-356-8085 *or* henryevansdesign.com   Builder's Advantage: Home Plans Volume 1

Government influence also pushes owners and design professionals to move toward this building process, because of mandatory requirements and building incentives or rebates (Ching 2012). Our Home Plans are designed and selected with environmentally friendly / energy efficient materials. We create construction documents that first and foremost comply with the prescriptive provisions of the International Residential Code (IRC). Our home plans select materials that maximize affordability and increase the building's life cycle.

We apply products that use renewable solar energy and place building systems purposefully, to allow effective air flow throughout the overall building space. For example, photovoltaic roofs or PV roofs, has increased tremendously with popularity and are typically known in application with solar roofs. For quite some time now, solar roofs have been widely accepted, because of its ability to generate electrical power from absorptions of the sun's rays. Current advancements of PV roofs integrate thin-film laminates with traditional roofing shingles. These models are flat-plate PV modules that resemble three-tab composite shingles. Within its application, typically they are installed just as shingles and integrated within the alignment of traditional shingles.

Because of this increased popularity, regulations have been put in place to standardize their placement, therefore photovoltaic shingles are to be installed per manufacturer's installation requirements (Ching 2012). Without question, flat plate PV modules that resemble three-tab composite shingles are considered to be a remarkable energy savings material, however this is only one application to the entire home or building envelope. Because energy efficiency and/or environmentally friendly building materials and systems are so important, each of Our Home Plans are designed and selected to incorporate environmentally friendly building materials and systems throughout the complete set of construction documents.

Builder's Advantage: Home Plans Volume 1   TO ORDER CALL: 1-888-356-8085 *or* henryevansdesign.com

BUILDER'S ADVANTAGE: Home Plans ™

*Our value package offering included with purchase of any home plan design.

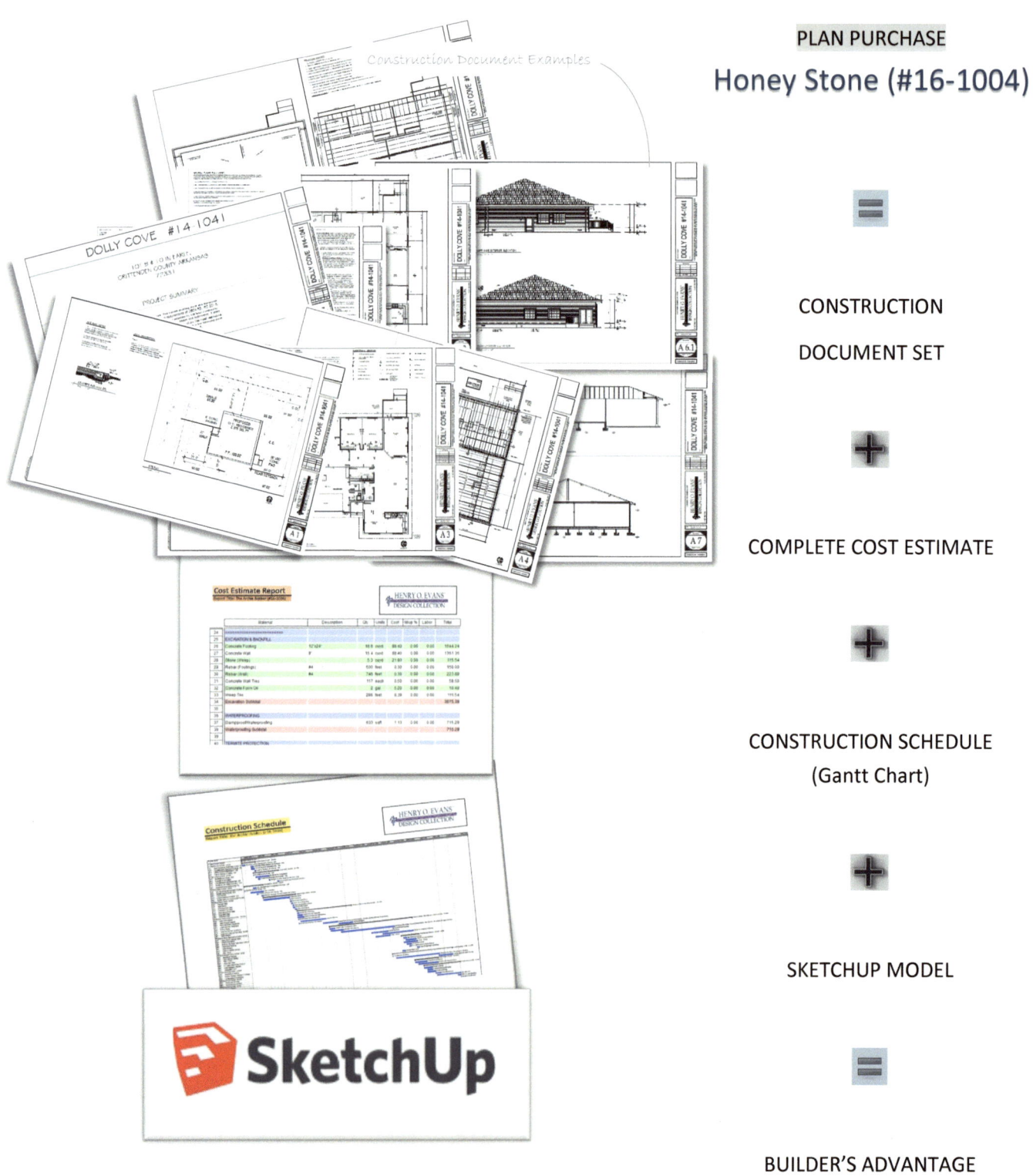

PLAN PURCHASE

Honey Stone (#16-1004)

=

CONSTRUCTION DOCUMENT SET

+

COMPLETE COST ESTIMATE

+

CONSTRUCTION SCHEDULE
(Gantt Chart)

+

SKETCHUP MODEL

=

BUILDER'S ADVANTAGE
(Value Package)

TO ORDER CALL: 1-888-356-8085   or   henryevansdesign.com   Builder's Advantage: Home Plans Volume 1

"The Honey Stone - HOEDC-16-1004" © 2017 Henry O. Evans Design Collection, LLC.

First Floor

Second Floor

Builder's Advantage: Home Plans Volume 1

Honey Stone

PLAN NUMBER: HOEDC-16-1004

BEDROOMS: 3

BATHS: 2 ½

WIDTH: 31'-0"

DEPTH: 51'-0"

1ST FLOOR: 807 sq. ft.

2nd FLOOR: 1355 sq. ft.

LIVING AREA: 2162 sq. ft.

FOUNDATION: Crawl Space

PRICES

1 SET: $740

5 SETS: $862

8 SETS: $937

VELLUM or PDF: $1073

CAD: $1864

A wonderful combination of siding elaborates the exterior of the this stunningly beautiful home. Distinctive brick & stone siding gives the facade warm texture and dimension.

TO ORDER CALL: 1-888-356-8085   or   henryevansdesign.com

Carefully sequenced rooms, permit the design to proceed freely and function properly throughout each space. This Brick & Stone styled home design, has a charming exterior that makes way for a spacious interior, rich with well-designed allocation and unique space assignment.

First Floor

Second Floor

Luxe Design Features:

- An impressive brick spiral column adorns the frontage with extravagant curb appeal and sensuous welcoming feel.
- Superb master bedroom & master bath and an open lounge area add spacious functionality throughout.
- Wood shutters and classic brick accents contribute gracefully, while hip-returned gables and Dutch-mansard roofs add support to the ambiance of a carefully formulated master-piece.

PLAN NAME: Honey Stone PLAN NUMBER: HOEDC-16-1004 PRICING: 1 SET: $740, 5 SETS: $862, 8 SETS: $937, VELLUM or PDF: $1073, CAD: $1864

TO ORDER CALL: 1-888-356-8085 *or* henryevansdesign.com

Builder's Advantage: Home Plans Volume 1

© "THE HONEY STONE, HOEDC-15-1001" (2017), HENRY O. EVANS DESIGN COLLECTION, LLC.

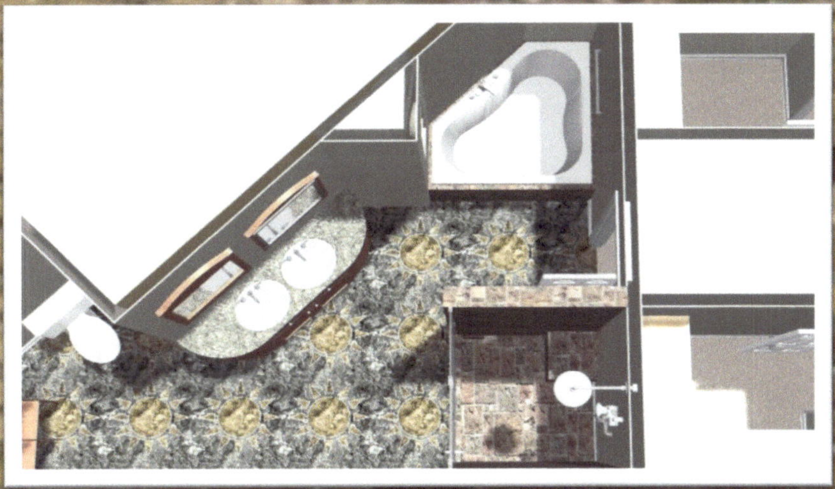

PLAN NAME: **Honey Stone** PLAN NUMBER: HOEDC-16-1004 PRICING: 1 SET: $740, 5 SETS: $862, 8 SETS: $937, VELLUM or PDF: $1073, CAD: $1864

Builder's Advantage: Home Plans Volume 1   TO ORDER CALL: 1-888-356-8085 *or* henryevansdesign.com

BUILDER'S ADVANTAGE: Home Plans ™

*Our value package offering included with purchase of any home plan design.

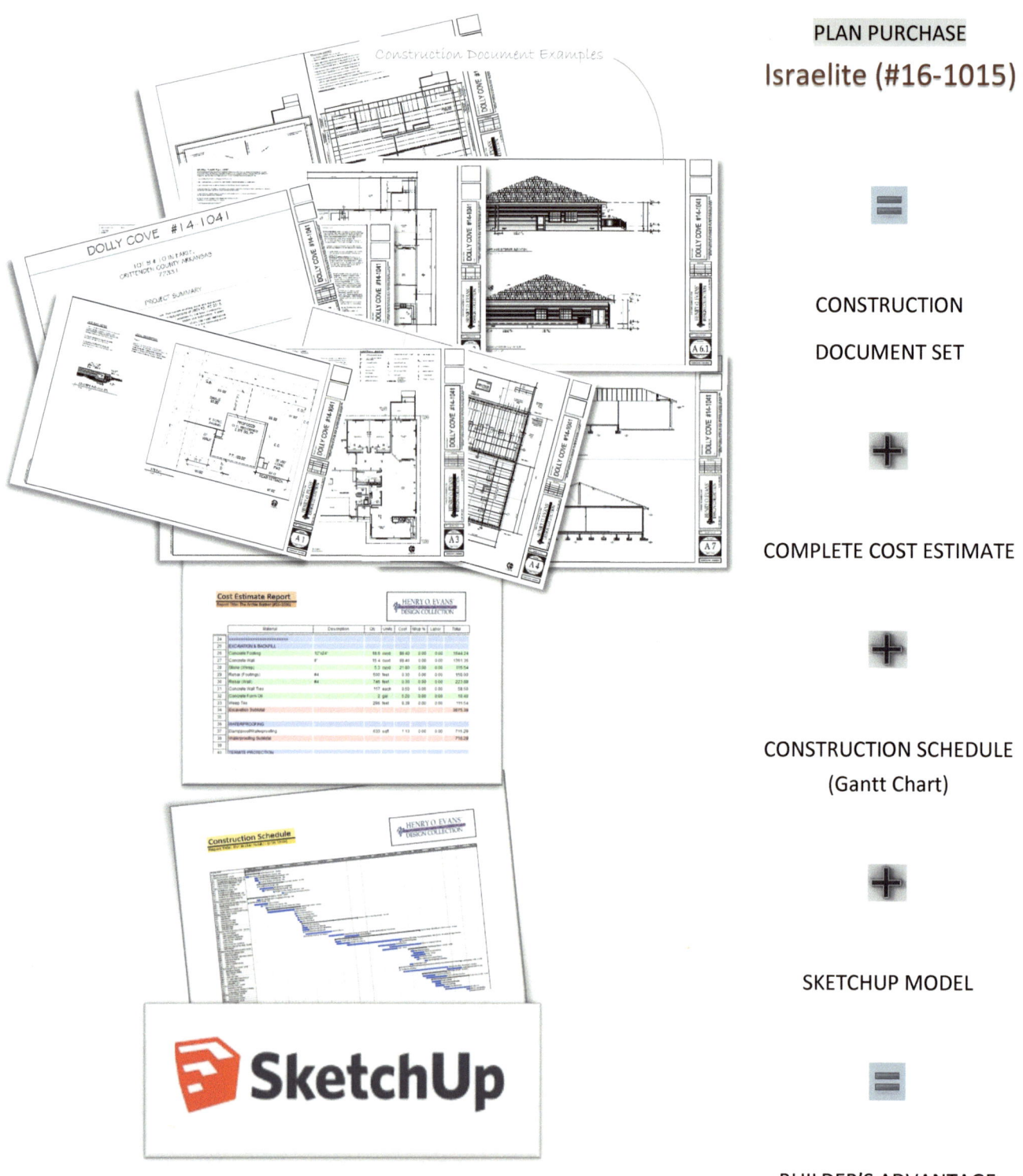

PLAN PURCHASE

Israelite (#16-1015)

=

CONSTRUCTION DOCUMENT SET

+

COMPLETE COST ESTIMATE

+

CONSTRUCTION SCHEDULE
(Gantt Chart)

+

SKETCHUP MODEL

=

BUILDER'S ADVANTAGE
(Value Package)

TO ORDER CALL: 1-888-356-8085   or   henryevansdesign.com

"The Israelite - HOEDC-16-1015" © 2017 Henry O. Evans Design Collection, LLC.

Israelite

PLAN NUMBER: HOEDC-16-1015

BEDROOMS: 3

BATHS: 2 ½

WIDTH: 31'-0"

DEPTH: 51'-0"

1ST FLOOR: 794 sq. ft.

2ND FLOOR: 1378 sq. ft.

LIVING AREA: 2172 sq. ft.

FOUNDATION: Crawl Space

PRICES

1 SET: $740

5 SETS: $862

8 SETS: $937

VELLUM or PDF: $1073

CAD: $1864

Intriguingly beautiful, is the first thought that comes to mind for this Mediterranean styled home design. It showcases powerful forms, both familiar and new that mesh together in harmonic design.

Builder's Advantage: Home Plans Volume 1   TO ORDER CALL: 1-888-356-8085 or henryevansdesign.com

Summer 2017 | Pg.51

Beautifully positioned columns, cantilevered bedrooms, and an array of sheik color-tones give the exterior of this design warm texture and dimension. Elegantly appointed exterior forms and smoothly transitioned interior rooms unite the whole family in this stunning home. Traditional yet eclectic, enchanting and yet cozy, this classically designed home ushers gracious entertaining and lavish living.

Luxe Design Features:

- Rich with history and primed with elements of a past era, this home design celebrates an easy transition of outdoor and interior spaces.
- An intricate entry sequence unfolds at the curb, appealing to the sensuous desire to venture within the interior.
- A warm and roomy floor plan, full functional kitchen, master-suite study & sitting area, and a gorgeous master bathroom.

PLAN NAME: **Israelite** PLAN NUMBER: HOEDC-16-1015 PRICING: 1 SET: $740, 5 SETS: $862, 8 SETS: $937, VELLUM or PDF: $1073, CAD: $1864

TO ORDER CALL: 1-888-356-8085 or *henryevansdesign.com*   Builder's Advantage: Home Plans Volume 1

© "THE ISRAELITE, HOEDC-16-1015" (2017), HENRY O. EVANS DESIGN COLLECTION, LLC.

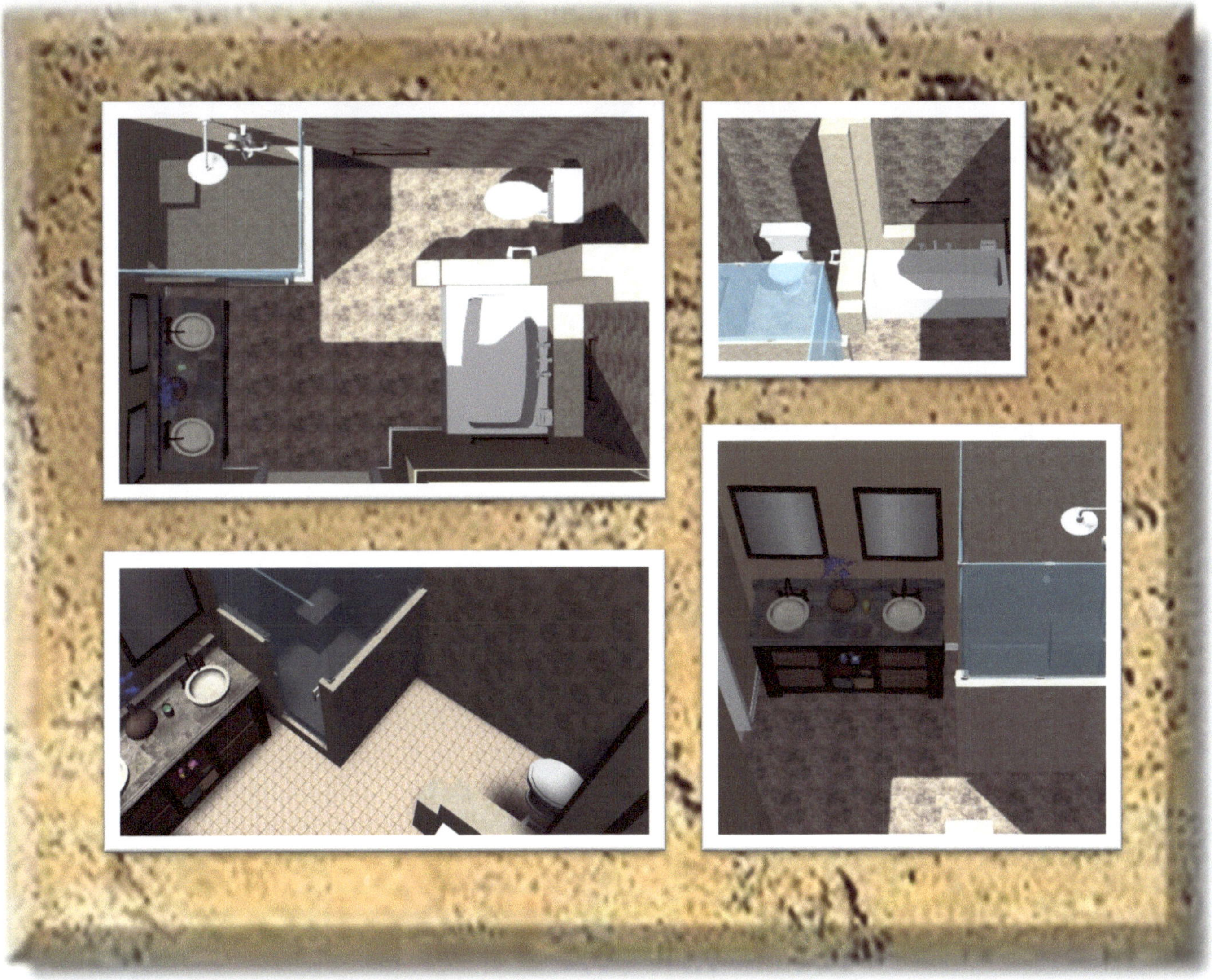

PLAN NAME: Israelite   PLAN NUMBER: HOEDC-16-1015   PRICING: 1 SET: $740, 5 SETS: $862, 8 SETS: $937, VELLUM or PDF: $1073, CAD: $1864

Builder's Advantage: Home Plans Volume 1   TO ORDER CALL: 1-888-356-8085   or   henryevansdesign.com

Factoring the Cost: Cost Estimating Tips

It is always important to count the cost, before building from any home plan or construction document.

By H. Evans

Q: I've found the home plan that I want, but how much will the materials cost?

Our home plans are packaged with complete cost estimates quantifying and itemizing all materials associated with the specific home design and/or construction documents. This addition to our home plan package saves the consumer time and money, that would normally have to be consumed, in order to allocate all associated design and construction related expenditures. Counting the cost is always important, before starting to build from any home plan and/or construction document. Although several companies today offer and sale several stock home plans and construction documents annually, they do not offer project management tools & techniques. Our solution to this problem is to combine home design and construction documentation with project management services. This combination will enable a value package offering that will aid our customers in the overall construction process. Over-looking key project cost and having erroneous estimates, could possibly cause construction projects to not meet their economic goals (Mubarak 2012).

TO ORDER CALL: 1-888-356-8085 *or* henryevansdesign.com

Builder's Advantage: Home Plans Volume 1

With our use of Building Information Modeling (BIM), we are able to extract the quantity takeoffs directly from the associated home plan model. Since the BIM applications are selected to coordinate each building part in real-time, the quantity take-offs are then directly extracted, therefore we believe, it minimizes erroneous expenditures that would normally be duplicated or left out using other traditional methods.

Because of our background in Project Management and Administration – Construction: We include with each of our stock home plans an actual construction schedule in the form of a Gantt chart in conjunction with a complete cost estimate. With these two techniques, scheduled tasks and resources are associated with time and cost, on a per project basis. Each Construction Cost Estimate Within Our Design Collection, is Specific to Each of Our Home Design and Construction Document Set, Individually. Because each project location is uniquely different, we employ the use of RS Means CostWorks, that allows each cost estimate to be adjusted per labor rates and material costs per region. A major point to remember when factoring the cost of your new construction project or new home, is that project budgeting and cost estimation are directly linked. This is extremely important to know, especially when it comes to cost control and project monitoring. Because the relationship between time and cost does not always parallel, this area will need steadfast applications that are able to make necessary adjustments as required (Pinto 2012).

Builder's Advantage: Home Plans Volume 1   TO ORDER CALL: 1-888-356-8085 *or* henryevansdesign.com

BUILDER'S ADVANTAGE: Home Plans ™

*Our value package offering included with purchase of any home plan design.

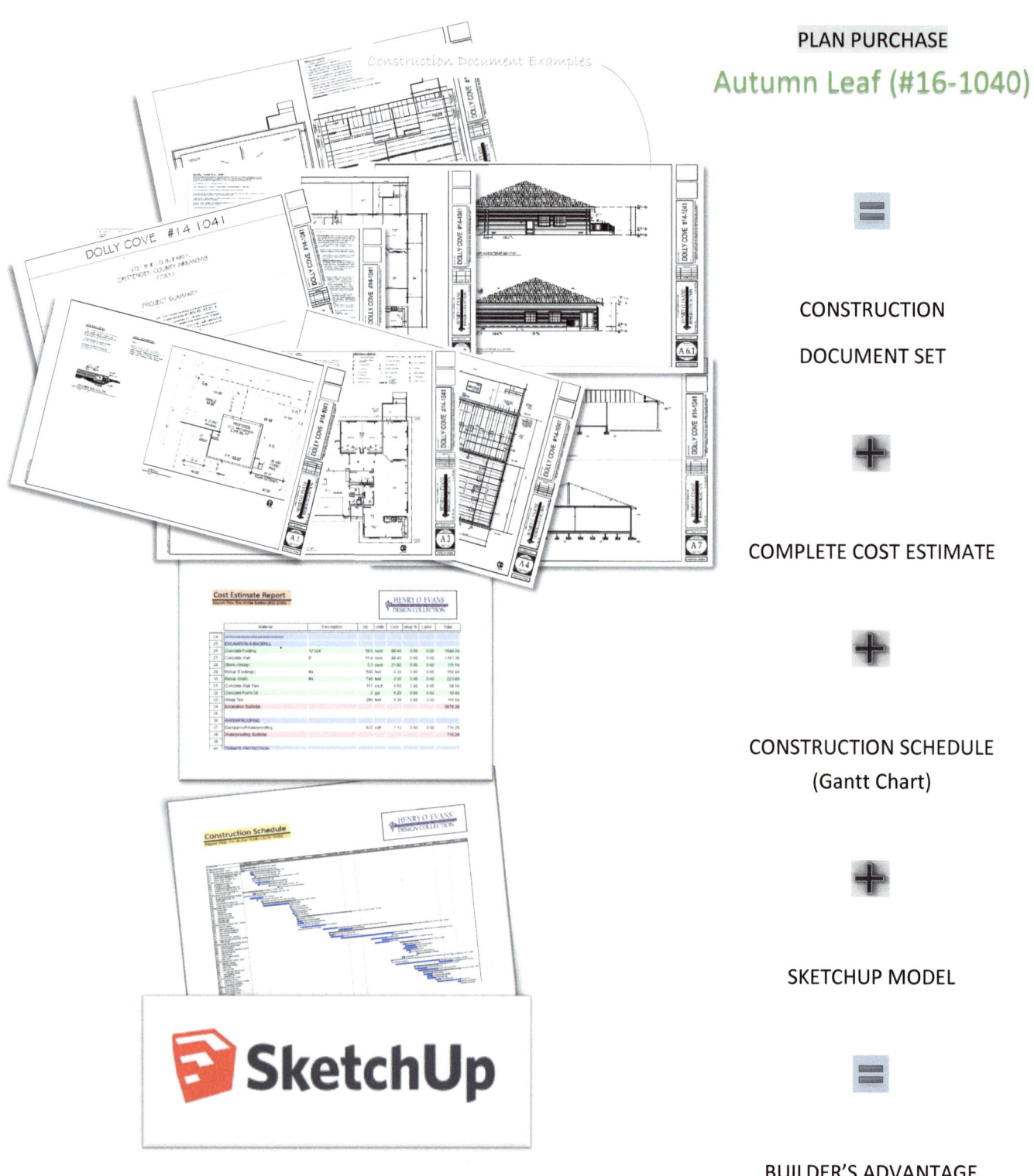

PLAN PURCHASE

Autumn Leaf (#16-1040)

=

CONSTRUCTION DOCUMENT SET

+

COMPLETE COST ESTIMATE

+

CONSTRUCTION SCHEDULE
(Gantt Chart)

+

SKETCHUP MODEL

=

BUILDER'S ADVANTAGE
(Value Package)

TO ORDER CALL: 1-888-356-8085 or henryevansdesign.com

Builder's Advantage: Home Plans Volume 1

"The Autumn Leaf - HOEDC-16-1040" © 2017 Henry O. Evans Design Collection, LLC.

Autumn Leaf

PLAN NUMBER: HOEDC-16-1040

BEDROOMS: 3

BATHS: 2 ½

WIDTH: 31'-0"

DEPTH: 51'-0"

1ST FLOOR: 833 sq. ft.

2ND FLOOR: 1200 sq. ft.

LIVING AREA: 2033 sq. ft.

FOUNDATION: Crawl Space

PRICES

1 SET: $740

5 SETS: $862

8 SETS: $937

VELLUM or PDF: $1073

CAD: $1864

Enjoy a traditional escape in this Mountain Home & Cabin styled master-piece. Life is easy, when your home retreat surrounds you every day. Prominent features include cozy covered deck, creative and delightful porch entry, and authentic cedar shake siding enhanced with cultured stone variations.

First Floor

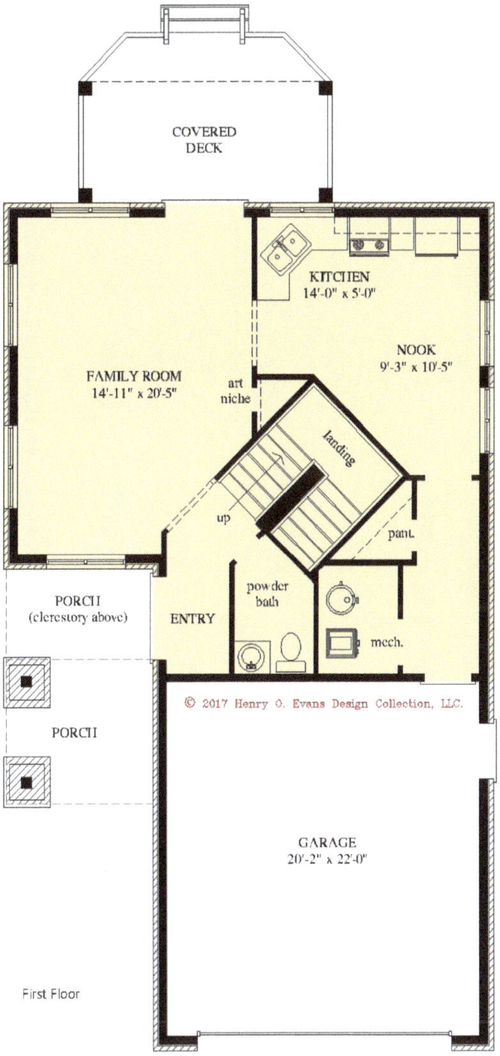

- COVERED DECK
- KITCHEN 14'-0" x 5'-0"
- FAMILY ROOM 14'-11" x 20'-5"
- NOOK 9'-3" x 10'-5"
- art niche
- landing / up
- pant.
- powder bath
- ENTRY
- mech.
- PORCH (clerestory above)
- PORCH
- GARAGE 20'-2" x 22'-0"

© 2017 Henry O. Evans Design Collection, LLC.

Second Floor

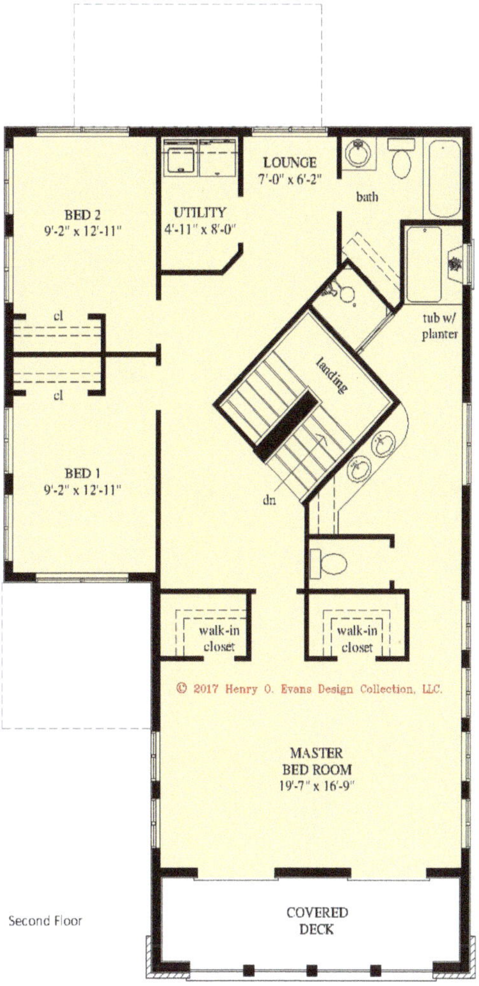

- LOUNGE 7'-0" x 6'-2"
- BED 2 9'-2" x 12'-11"
- UTILITY 4'-11" x 8'-0"
- bath
- cl / cl
- tub w/ planter
- BED 1 9'-2" x 12'-11"
- landing / dn
- walk-in closet
- walk-in closet
- MASTER BED ROOM 19'-7" x 16'-9"
- COVERED DECK

© 2017 Henry O. Evans Design Collection, LLC.

Builder's Advantage: Home Plans Volume 1   TO ORDER CALL: 1-888-356-8085   or   henryevansdesign.com

Exposed wood gives a country feel of classic craftmanship that mix gently with new-age technology. Although it has a gracefully crafted exterior, it is also, equipped with interesting space placement through-out the interior. It's rich texture and crafted details incorporate a calm artistry of shapes to suit any timbered location.

First Floor

Second Floor

Luxe Design Features:

- An invigorating entry gives way to a unique family room, art niche, kitchen and dining area.
- Its spacious master bedroom, walk-in closets, and attractive master bath with camouflage cabinet finish.
- Beautifully positioned covered deck, to take in all the outdoor views.

PLAN NAME: Autumn Leaf PLAN NUMBER: HOEDC-16-1040 PRICING: 1 SET: $740, 5 SETS: $862, 8 SETS: $937, VELLUM or PDF: $1037, CAD: $1864

TO ORDER CALL: 1-888-356-8085 *or* henryevansdesign.com

Builder's Advantage: Home Plans Volume 1

© "THE AUTUMN LEAF, HOEDC-16-1040" (2017), HENRY O. EVANS DESIGN COLLECTION, LLC.

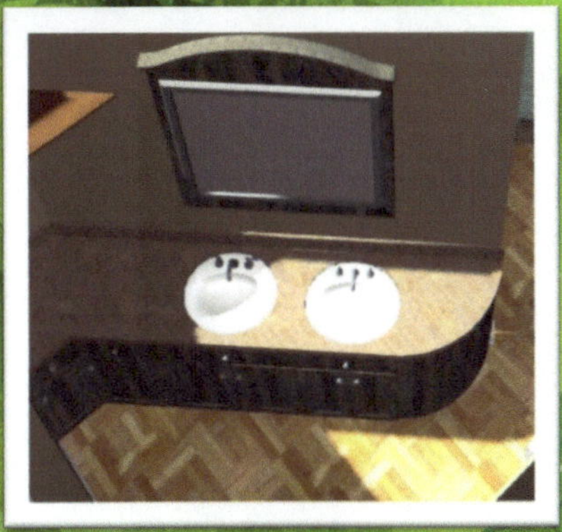

PLAN NAME: Autumn Leaf   **PLAN NUMBER:** HOEDC-16-1040   **PRICING:** 1 SET: $740, 5 SETS: $862, 8 SETS: $937, VELLUM or PDF: $1073, CAD: $1864

Builder's Advantage: Home Plans Volume 1   TO ORDER CALL: 1-888-356-8085   *or*   henryevansdesign.com

10 Reasons to Choose Narrow Lot Home Plans

By H. Evans

1. First Time Home Buyer You're looking for an efficient affordable, and preferential route, with the experience of building your own home.

2. Better Land Usage To efficiently allocate multiple homes in any given land tract.

3. Urban Areas You're looking to build home in expansive urban areas.

4. Land is Becoming Scarcer To implement efficient land usage.

5. Narrow Lot Configuration Your lot has a narrow configuration.

6. Benefit from Most Usable Space You want to get the most efficient design within a usable space.

7. You Have Narrow Land Tracts You're looking to utilize the narrow land tracts you currently own.

8. Efficient Lifestyle You're looking to live more efficiently and use fewer space requirements.

9. Cost Effective Design You're looking for more cost-effective design styles with several amenities.

10. More Creative Uses of Space You're looking to benefit from more effective and creative space allocation, coupled with quality design.

BUILDER'S ADVANTAGE: Home Plans ™

*Our value package offering included with purchase of any home plan design.

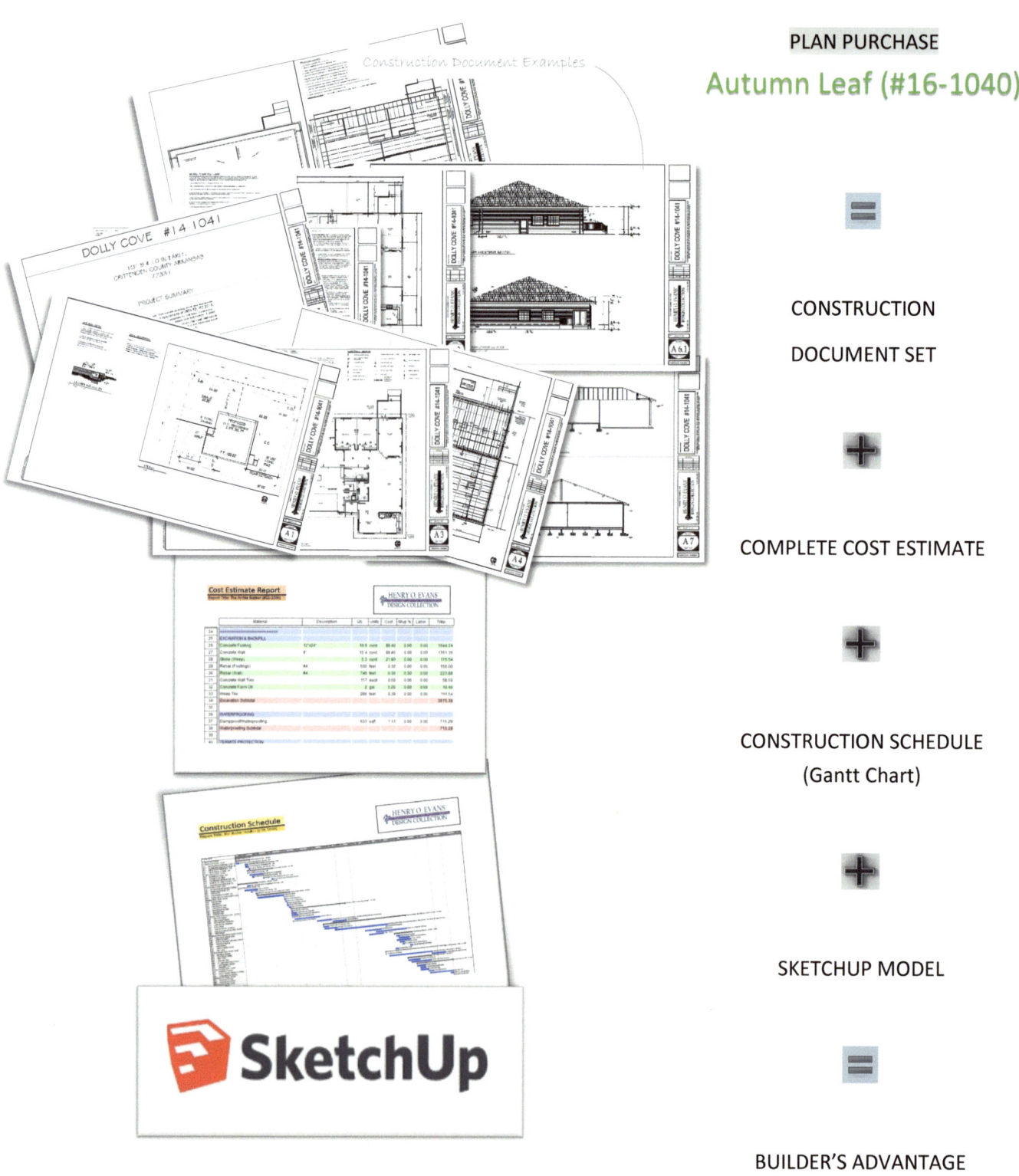

PLAN PURCHASE

Autumn Leaf (#16-1040)

=

CONSTRUCTION DOCUMENT SET

+

COMPLETE COST ESTIMATE

+

CONSTRUCTION SCHEDULE
(Gantt Chart)

+

SKETCHUP MODEL

=

BUILDER'S ADVANTAGE
(Value Package)

TO ORDER CALL: 1-888-356-8085 or henryevansdesign.com

Builder's Advantage: Home Plans Volume 1

"The Cocoa Cabana - HOEDC-08-1024" © 2017 Henry O. Evans Design Collection, LLC.

Cocoa Cabana

PLAN NUMBER: HOEDC-08-1024

BEDROOMS: 3

BATHS: 2 ½

WIDTH: 31'-0"

DEPTH: 51'-0"

1ST FLOOR: 802 sq. ft.

2ND FLOOR: 1257 sq. ft.

LIVING AREA: 2059 sq. ft.

FOUNDATION: Crawl Space

PRICES

1 SET: $740

5 SETS: $862

8 SETS: $937

VELLUM or PDF: $1073

CAD: $1864

Lavish living is celebrated in this Coastal styled sensation, ideal for those living near impressive landscapes.

Builder's Advantage: Home Plans Volume 1   TO ORDER CALL: 1-888-356-8085   or   henryevansdesign.com

This magnificent design was Inspired by living in Key West and traveling the American Archipelago from the Florida Keys to Miami. It has a lovely forecourt that establishes a progressive and exciting passage to its entry. As you visualize each detail, I'm sure you'll agree that sheer opulence is everywhere in this sheik waterfront home design.

First Floor

- FAMILY ROOM 20'-2" x 13'-11"
- KITCHEN 12'-8" x 9'-4"
- NOOK 9'-0" x 9'-8"
- powder bath
- mech.
- up
- landing
- PORCH
- GARAGE 20'-2" x 22'-0"
- PORTICO

© 2017 Henry O. Evans Design Collection, LLC.

Second Floor

- MASTER BED ROOM 18'-2" x 14'-2"
- master bath
- counter
- walk-in closet
- bath
- wet bar
- hall way
- dn
- landing
- SITTING ROOM 11'-8" x 11'-8"
- BED 1 9'-11" x 11'-7"
- BED 2 9'-11" x 11'-7"
- OPEN DECK
- OPEN DECK

© 2017 Henry O. Evans Design Collection, LLC.

Luxe Design Features:

- This home reflects the design difference of Pristinely Innovative, with its smooth stucco walls, distinctive newels, and tropical railings that merge gracefully, creating a spectacular plan that is both cutting edge and comfortable.
- Full paneled sliding doors along with tall windows articulate the spacious sun deck, allowing prevailing summer breezes to find their way through a carefully situated interior.
- Its beautiful open kitchen and spacious master suite. Also, its exquisite sitting room releases to the lovely open deck.

PLAN NAME: Cocoa Cabana   PLAN NUMBER: HOEDC-08-1024   PRICING: 1 SET: $740, 5 SETS: $862, 8 SETS: $937, VELLUM or PDF: $1073, CAD: $1864

TO ORDER CALL: 1-888-356-8085 or henryevansdesign.com   Builder's Advantage: Home Plans Volume 1

© "THE COCOA COBANA, HOEDC-08-1024" (2017), HENRY O. EVANS DESIGN COLLECTION, LLC.

PLAN NAME: Cocoa Cabana **PLAN NUMBER:** HOEDC-08-1024 **PRICING:** 1 SET: $740, 5 SETS: $862, 8 SETS: $937, VELLUM or PDF: $1073, CAD: $1864

Builder's Advantage: Home Plans Volume 1

TO ORDER CALL: 1-888-356-8085 *or* *henryevansdesign.com*

Summer 2017 | Pg.65

Make it Your Own, Customize the Design

" CHANGE and MODIFICATION PROCESS "

Because we can make almost any change or changes to a floor plan, we look forward to accomodating the needs of our clients rquest! If you are needing to simply bring plans up to the building codes in your area, to satisfy the requirements of the local jurisdiction, you will need to purchase the reproducible vellum or CAD for the modifications to be permitted due to copyright law.

1 Select the Plan That Fits Your Needs, As you browse through our home plan publication or website, select the plan that most closely aligns with your desired needs. Once selected order your desired plan via phone or online at the address at the bottom of this publication.

2 Submit Modification Request, Once selected order your desired plan via phone or online at the address at the bottom of this publication and submit desired changes with order.

3 Calculate Cost to Make Changes, Once we have received the modofication request, we will calculate the cost to make changes. If chages to any home plan supercedes more than half the entire design, we recommend you order a custom home design. Our team will then work closely with you to create and design the home of your dreams.

" CATEGORIES of CHANGES and MODIFICATIONS "

Minor, changes consist of changing exterior finishes and materials, resizing and/or moving doors and windows, and altering non-load bearing walls.

Average, changes consist of foundation changes, adding a fireplace, enlarging kitchen or bathrooms, roof pitches, adding a room, garage or porch.

Extreme, changes consist of changes that total more than half the origianl design and for this amount of changes we recommend considering custom design options.

Resources and References

IMAGES of FLOOR PLANS and INTERIOR / EXTERIOR RENDERINGS

Photos and images of home designs exterior may vary with floor plan image and construction documents, due to varying floor elevations with number of steps ect.. Because of regional frost depth and flood zone ratings, floor elevations can differ depending on building locality.

All images of floor plans and interior / exterior renderings of home designs are copyright registered. and property of Henry O. Evans and Henry O. Evans Design Collection, LLC.

Henry O. Evans Design Collection, LLC.
P.O. Box 85, Springfield, Mo. 65801
Toll free 1-888-356-8085

PHOTOS FROM ARTICLES SECTIONS

Photos from articles sections have been provided from online lesson plan tutorials, from Bachelor of Science Program for Project Management and Administration – Construction.
Coutesy of ITT Technical Institute.

ARTICLE CITATIONS

Ching, F. K., Winkel, S. R. (2012-06-25). ***Building Codes Illustrated: A Guide to Understanding the 2012 International Building Code, 4th Edition.***

Pinto, J. K., & Venkataraman, R. R. (2013). ***Cost and Value Management in Projects.*** Hoboken, N.J: Wiley.

Project management, I. (2013). ***A Guide to the Project Management Body of Knowledge*** (PMBOK Guide). Newton Square, Pennsylvania: Project Management Institute.

Mubarak, Saleh A., Ph.D. (2012). Means. ***How to Estimate with RSMeans Data, 4th Edition,*** 4th Edition. John Wiley & Sons P&T, 4/3/16. Vital Source Bookshelf Online.

American Institute of Architects,, In Hall, D. J., & Magnum Group,. (2013). ***Architectural Graphic Standards.***

Pinto, J. K. (2012). ***Project Management: Achieving Competitive Advantage.***

TO ORDER CALL: 1-888-356-8085 or henryevansdesign.com

Our Builder's Advantage value package offering includes:

Construction Document Set of specified home design,

Cost Estimate of specific home design,

Note: each home planning service listed above can be ordered individually or separate from value package, call to inquire within for further details and additional questions.

Construction Scheduling in the form of a Gantt chart, *and*

Sketchup Model to view home design in real-time

Glossary

This glossary is composed to assist in clarifying the concepts within this Plan Book. Words that are included are based on the concepts of building design and construction, residential contracting, and project management. For reasons of space, many words used now have other meanings not defined here.

Acceptance Criteria
Those criteria including performance requirements and essential conditions, which must be met before project deliverables are accepted.

Activity
A component of work performed during a project.

Activity Duration
The time in calendar units between the start and finish of a schedule activity.

Activity List
A documented tabulation of a schedule activities that shows the activity description, activity identifier, and a sufficiently detailed scope of work description so project team members understand what work is to be performed.

Acquire Project Team
The process of confirming manpower resource availability and obtaining the team necessary to complete project assignments.

Adjustable Rate Mortgage (ARM)
A mortgage in which the interest rate is adjusted periodically up or down, usually once or twice a year.

Annual Percentage Rate (APR)
The total amount of your mortgage loan package (interest, loan fees, points, or other charges.) expressed as a percentage of the loan amount. The APR is usually slightly higher than the actual interest rate.

Appraised Value
An estimate of the value of property, such as a house.

Approved Change Request
A change request that has been processed through the integrated change control process and approved.

Backward Pass
The calculation of late finish dates and late start dates for the uncompleted portions of all schedule activities. Determined by working backwards through the schedule network logic from the project's end date.

Balloon (Payment) Mortgage
Usually a short-term fixed-rate loan, it involves small payments for a certain period of time and one large payment for the remaining amount of the principle at a time specified in the contract.

Baseline
An approved plan for a project, plus or minus approved changes. It is compared to actual performance to determine if performance is within acceptable variance thresholds. Generally, refers to the current baseline. Usually used with a modifier (e.g. cost performance baseline, schedule baseline, performance measurement baseline, technical baseline).

Binder
Money given by a buyer to a seller as part of the purchase price to bind a transaction or ensure payment (also called earnest money).

Brainstorming
A general data gathering and creativity technique that can be used to identify risk, ideas, or solutions to issues by using a group of team members or subject-matter experts.

Brick Veneer
Brick used in lieu of siding.

Bridge Loan
A short-term loan to bridge the time between the purchase of one house and the seller of another.

Budget
The approved estimate for the project or any work breakdown structure component or any schedule activity.

Camber
a slight crown or arch in a horizontal structural member, such as a beam or truss, to compensate for deflection under a load.

Change Request
Request to expand or reduce the project scope, modify policies, processes, plans, or procedures, modify costs or budgets, or revise schedules.

Chase
A channel built into a wall or ceiling to hold wiring, plumbing, or vents.

Clear Title
A title (a proof of ownership) of any property (land, auto, house) that is free of liens, mortgages, judgements, or any other encumbrance.

Closing
The meeting between the buyer, seller, and lender or their agents where the property legally changes hands.

Closing Costs
Costs the buyer must pay at the time of closing in addition to the down payment, including points, mortgage insurance premium, homeowner's insurance, prepayments for property taxes, and so on. Closing costs usually average 2 to 4 percent of the loan amount.

Closing Processes
Those processes performed to finalize all activities across all Project Management Process Groups to formally close the project or phase.

Color Run
Materials produced using the same batch of dye, such as bricks, carpet, or paint. Subsequent batches may vary in color.

Column
A vertical structural member.

Cornice
The horizontal projection of a roof overhang at the eaves, consisting of lookout, soffit, and fascia.

Communication Management Plan
The document that describes: the communications needs and expectations for the project; how and in what format information will be communicated; when and where each communication will be made; and who is responsible for providing each type of communication. The communication management plan is contained in, or is a subsidiary plan of, the project management plan.

Constraint
The state, quality, or sense of being restricted to a given course of action or inaction. An applicable restriction or limitation, either internal or external to a project, which will affect the performance of the project or a process. For example, a schedule constraint is any limitation or restraint placed on the project schedule that affects when a schedule activity can be scheduled and is usually in the form of fixed imposed dates.

Contract
A contract is a mutually binding agreement that obligates the seller to provide the specified product or service or result and obligates the buyer to pay for it.

Contract Price
A pre-agreed set price for a service or product.

Control Costs
The process of monitoring the status of the project to update the project to update the project budget and managing changes to cost baseline.

Control Scope
The process of monitoring the status of the project and product scope and managing changes to the scope baseline.

Course
A row of bricks.

Cost Management

The document that sets out the format and establishes the activities and criteria for planning, structuring, and controlling the project costs. The cost management plan is contained in, or is a subsidiary plan of, the project management plan.

Crawl Space

[1] An area under a floor or roof where there is insufficient space to stand up. [2] The area bounded by foundation walls, first-floor joists, and the ground in a house with no basement.

Crashing

A specific type of project schedule compression technique performed by taking action to decrease the total project schedule duration after analyzing a number of alternatives to determine how to get the maximum schedule duration compression for the least additional cost. Typical approaches for crashing a schedule include reducing schedule activity durations and increasing the assignment of resources on schedule activities.

Critical Path

Generally, but not always, the sequence of schedule activities that determines the duration of the project. It is the longest path through the project.

Deed Restrictions

Encumbrances placed on a piece of real estate and filed as a matter of record that restrict or prevent certain uses of the property.

Deliverable

Any unique and verifiable product, result, or capability to perform a service that must be produced to complete a process, phase, or project. Often used more narrowly in reference to an external deliverable, which is a deliverable that is subject to approval by the project sponsor or customer.

Dormer

A structure with its own roof projecting from a sloping roof, typically to accommodate a vertical window.

Down Payment

Money paid up front to make up the difference between the purchase price and the mortgage amount.

Draw

A disbursement of money representing a portion or percentage of the entire amount.

Dry-in

The stage in construction when walls, roof, and windows are in place so that the interior of the building is protected from rain and snow. *See also, rough-in.*

Drywall

Used to finish interior walls; sheetrock is a commonly used term.

Eave

The part of a roof that projects beyond its supporting walls.

Elevations

Drawings of the exterior of a structure.

Equity

The difference between what is owed on a property and what it is worth. It equals the percentage of the mortgage that has been paid off, and can be used as collateral for a home equity loan.

Escrow

An account held by the lender into which the home owner pays money for tax or insurance payments and for binders to be held pending loan closing.

Fascia (Fascia Boards)

The flat horizontal boards at the edge of the roof. A vertical board nailed to the lower ends of rafters that form part of a cornice.

Float

Also called slack.

Flue
A channel for the passage of hot gasses and smoke.

Footing
A concrete structure below the frost line supporting the foundation or piers of a house.

Forecast
An estimate or prediction of conditions and events in the project's future based on information and knowledge available at the time of the forecast. The information is based on the project's past performance and expected future performance, and includes information that could impact the project in the future, such as estimate at completion and estimate to complete.

Forward pass
The calculation of the early start and early finish dates for the uncompleted portions of all network activities.

Foundation
The buildings' structural support below the first-floor construction, that rests on the footing and transfers the weight of the building to the soil.

Framing
The construction of the skeleton of a house, including walls, floors, ceiling, and roof.

Frame Construction
Using wood, as opposed to brick, block, concrete, or steel, for building walls, ceilings and roofs.

French Drains
Pipes placed around or beneath a structure to provide a positive drainage.

Frost Line
The depth in the earth at which the warmth of the earth prevents or the formation of frost.

Fur Out
To make wall or ceiling deeper to provide a chase.

Gable
The triangle part of an end wall between the eaves and ridge of a house with a peaked roof.

Gable Roof
A roof shape characterized by two sections of roof of constant slope that meet at a ridge; peaked roof.

Gantt Chart
A graphic display of schedule-related information. In the typical bar chart, schedule activities or work breakdown structure components are listed down the left side of the chart, dates are shown across the top, and activity durations are shown as date-placed horizontal bars.

Grade
1. A designation of quality, especially of lumber and plywood.
2. Ground level. Also, the slope of the ground on a building site.

Heat Pump
An electrical appliance for heating and cooling a building. In the heating phase, it draws heat from the outside air (even cold air) and transfers it to the inside of a house or other building. Acts as an air conditioner in the summer.

Hip
The outside angle where two adjacent sections of roof meet at a diagonal. The opposite of a valley.

Hip roof
A roof shape characterized by four or more sections of constant slope, all of which run from a uniform eave height to the ridge.

HVAC
The heating, ventilating, air-conditioning system of a building.

Identify Risks
The process of determining which risks may affect the project and documenting their characteristics.

Identify Stakeholders
The process of identifying all people or organizations impacted by the project, and documenting relevant information regarding their interests, involvement, and impact on project success.

Interim Financing

A short-term loan that is generally converted to a long-term loan later.

International Building Code (IBC)

The building code established in 2000 by the international Code Council (ICC) to cover all buildings except one-and-two-family dwellings and multiple single-family dwellings, not further than three stories in height.

International Residential Code (IRC)

The International Code Council's (ICC) building code that covers all one-and two-family dwellings and multiple single-family dwellings not more than three stories in height.

Invitation for Bid (IFB)

Generally, this term is equivalent to request for proposal. However, in some application areas, it may have a narrower or more specific meaning.

Joists

Small horizontal timbers to support a floor or ceiling.

Lag

A modification of a logical relationship that directs a delay in the successor activity. For example, in a finish-to-start dependency with a ten-day lag, the successor activity cannot start until ten days after the predecessor activity has finished.

Lead

A modification of a logical relationship that allows an acceleration of the successor activity. For example, in a finish-to-start dependency with a ten-day lead, the successor activity can start ten days before the predecessor activity has finished. A negative lead is equivalent to a positive lag.

Leveling

See resource leveling.

Load-Bearing Capability

The amount of weight a substance can withstand without braking or bending beyond its design. Used to describe soil, steel, or wood.

Log

A document used to record and describe or denote selected items identified during execution of a process or activity. Usually used with a modifier, such as issue, quality control, action, or defect.

Lot Subordination

A process of buying land by which the owner takes a note in lieu of payment and legally takes an interest in that land secondary to a party with primary interest such as a savings and loan.

Manager's Contract

A contract with a general contractor by which the latter agrees to act as a manager to construct your house. Under such a contract, you can remain the primary general contractor.

Mansard Roof

A type of roof with two slopes on each of four sides, the lower slope much steeper than the upper and ending at a constant eave height.

Market Value

The highest price that a buyer would pay and the lowest price a seller would accept on a property. Market value may be different from the price a property could be sold for at a given time.

Milestone

A significant point or event in the project.

Molding

The interior trim around windows, doors, ceilings, and other features in a house.

Mortgage Insurance

Money paid to insure the mortgage when the down payment is less than 20 percent.

Network Path
Any continuous series of schedule activities connected with logical relationships in a project schedule network diagram.

Nominal size
The rounded-off, simplified dimensional name given to lumber. For example, a piece of lumber whose actual size is $1^{1/2}" \times 3^{1/2}"$ is given the more convenient, nominal designation of 2" x 4".

Note
A written acknowledgment of a debt, such as a promissory note.

O.C. (On Center)
Before lumber widths were standardized, carpenters measured from the center of one stud (or rafter or joists) to the center of the next. Commonly used to mean inches apart.

Origination Fee
The fee charged by a leader to prepare loan documents, make credit checks, inspect, and sometimes appraise property, usually computed as a percentage of the face value of the loan.

Overhang
The part of a roof that extends beyond supporting walls.

Partition
An interior wall that divides a building into rooms or areas.

Panel Box
Electrical panel. A metal box containing circuit breakers.

Percolation (perc) Test
Tests to determine if the soil on a piece of land can support a septic system.

Pier
A vertical structural support. Usually a masonry or metal column that supports the house, porch, or deck.

Pitch
The slope of a roof.

Pitch (of roof)
How steeply the roof rises per foot of horizontal travel. An average pitch of 6/12, or 6 inches of rise per foot.

Pitch Angle
The vertical angle on the end of a rafter that represents the pitch of a roof.

Plan Communications
The process of determining project stakeholder information needs and defining a communication approach.

Plan Risk Management
The process of defining how to conduct risk management activities for a project.

Ponting Up
Touching the minor imperfections and damage in new walls after they have been primed but before final painting occurs.

Points (Loan Discount Points)
Prepaid interest assessed at closing by the lender. Each point is equal to 1 percent of the loan amount (e.g., two points on a $1,000,000 mortgage cost $2,000). The purpose of paying points is to obtain a lower interest rate on the mortgage.

Polyethylene
Plastic film used on home construction to provide a moisture barrier.

Pythagorean Theorem
The theorem that the sum of the squares of the lengths of the sides of a right triangle is equal to the square of the length of the hypotenuse.

Procurement Management Plan

The document that describes how procurement processes from developing procurement documentation through contract closure will be managed.

Project

A temporary endeavor undertaken to create a unique product, service, or result.

Project Management

The application of knowledge, skills, tools, and techniques to project activities to meet the project requirements.

Project Management Body of Knowledge (PMBOK)

An inclusive term that describes the sum of knowledge within the profession of project management. As with other professionals, such as law, medicine, and accounting, the body of knowledge includes proven traditional practices that are widely applied and innovative practices that are emerging in the profession. The body of knowledge includes both published and unpublished materials. This body of knowledge is constantly evolving. PMI's PMBOK guide identifies that subset of the project management body of knowledge that is generally recognized as good practice.

Project Management Plan

A formal, approved document that defines how the project is executed, monitored, and controlled. It may be a summary or detailed and may be composed of one or more subsidiary management plans and other planning documents.

Project Management Team

The members of the project team who are directly involved in project management activities. On some smaller projects, the project management team may include virtually all of the project team members.

Project Manager (PM)

The person assigned by the performing organization to achieve the project objectives.

Project Phase

A collection of logically related project activities, usually culminating in the completion of a major deliverable. Project phases are mainly completed sequentially, but can overlap in some project situations. A project phase is a component of a project life cycle. A project phase is not a project Management Process Group.

Project Scope

The work that must be performed to deliver a product, service, or result with the specified features and functions.

Project Scope Statement

The narrative description of the project scope, including major deliverables, project assumptions, project constraints, and a description of work, that provides a documented basis for making future project decisions and for confirming or developing a mutual understanding of project scope among the stakeholders.

Quote

A guaranteed price in advance.

Recording Fee

The fee charged to record legal documents in a place of permanent records, such as a county court house.

Reinforcing Rod

A steel rod placed in concrete to increase to increase the strength of the concrete. Also known as rebar.

Request for Information (RFI)

A type of procurement document whereby the buyer requests a potential seller to provide various pieces of information related to a product or service or seller capability.

Request for Proposal (RFP)

A type of procurement document used to request proposals from prospective sellers of products or services. In some application areas, it may have a narrower or more specific meaning.

Reserve

A provision in the project management plan to mitigate cost and/or schedule risk. Often used with a modifier (e.g., management reserve, contingency reserve) to provide further detail on what types of risk are meant to be mitigated.

Resource

Skilled human resources (specific disciplines either individually or in crews or teams), equipment, services, supplies, commodities, material, budgets, or funds.

Resource Leveling

Any form of schedule network analysis in which scheduling decisions (start and finish dates) are driven by resources constraints (e.g., limited resource availability or difficult-to-manage changes in resources availability levels).

Rough-in

The installation of wiring, plumbing, or heat ducts in the walls, floors, or ceilings before the walls, floors, or ceilings are covered with drywall, plaster or paneling. *See also, dry-in.*

Root Cause Analysis

Analytical technique used to determine the basic underlying reason that causes a variance or a defect or a risk. A root cause may underlie more than on variance or defect or risk.

Saw Service

Temporary electrical service used during construction.

Second Mortgage

The pledging of property to a lender as a security for payment, using property that has already been pledged for a loan.

Septic System

Means of disposing sewage in the ground.

Schedule Baseline

A specific version of the schedule model used to compare actual results to the plan to determine if preventive or corrective action is needed to meet the project objectives.

Scope

The sum of the products, services, and results to be provided as a project.

Scope Creep

Adding features and functionality (project scope) without addressing the effects on time, costs, and resources, or without customer approval.

Slab

A poured concrete foundation for a garage or other structure with no basement.

Slack

Also called float.

Specification

A document that specifies, in a complete, precise, verifiable manner, the requirements, design, behavior, or other characteristics of a system, component, product, result, or service and, often, the procedures for determining whether these provisions have been satisfied. Examples are: requirement specification, design specification, product specification, and test specification.

Specifications (spec's)

A listing of all materials to be used in building or renovating a structure.

Square

The amount of roofing material needed to cover 100 square feet of roof.

Soffit

The underside of a roof overhang.

Staking

Placing stakes in the ground prior to building to show the location of the corners of the house.

Stakeholder
Person or organization (e.g., customer, sponsor, performing organization, or the public) that is actively involved in the project, or whose interests may be positively or negatively affected by execution or completion of the project. A stakeholder may also exert influence over the project and its deliverables.

Start Date
A point in time associated with a schedule activity's start, usually qualified by one of the following: actual, planned, estimated, scheduled, early, late, target, baseline, or current.

Statement of Work (SOW)
A narrative description of products,

Services, or results to be supplied.

Strengths, Weakness, Opportunities, and Threats (SWOT) Analysis
This information gathering technique examines the project from the perspective of each project's strengths, weaknesses, opportunities, and threats to increase the breadth of the risks considered by risk management.

Take-off
The compilation of a list of materials used for a particular phase of construction, such as the number of bricks or the number and sizes of windows. Also called a schedule of materials, it can often be prepared by a lumberyard or other supplier.

Test Boring
Sample of the soil upon which a structure is to be built to determine what weight the soil upon which a structure is to be built to determine what weight the soil can carry.

Technique
A defined systematic procedure employed by a human resource to perform an activity to produce a product or result or deliver a service, and that may employ one or more tools.

Time and Material (T&M) Contract
A type of contract that is a hybrid contractual arrangement containing aspects of both cost reimbursable and fixed-price contracts. Time and material contracts resemble cost-reimbursable type arrangements in that they have no definitive end, because the full value of the arrangement is not defined at the time of the award. Thus, time and material contracts can grow in contract value as if they were cost-reimbursable-type arrangements. Conversely, time and material arrangements can also resemble fixed-price arrangements. For example, the unit rates are preset by the buyer and seller, when both parties agree on the rates for the category of senior engineers.

Title Insurance
An insurance policy that protects the owner of real estate from any loss due to defects in his title.

Topographical Plat (topo)
A drawing showing the surface features of property.

Transit
A surveying instrument used to measure horizontal angles, levelness, and vertical depth.

Triggers
Indications that a risk has occurred or is about to occur. Triggers may be discovered in the risk identification process and watched in the risk monitoring and control process. Triggers are sometimes called risk symptoms or warning signs.

Trim Out
The stage of construction when final trim items are installed – toilets, moldings, light fixtures, and so on.

Unsecured Loan
A loan which no material possessions are pledged as security for repayment.

Value Engineering
An approach used to optimize project life cycle costs, save time, increase profits, improve quality, expand market share, solve problems, and/or use resources more effectively.

Virtual Team

A group of persons with a shared objective who fulfill their roles with little or no time spent meeting face to face. Various forms of technology are often used to facilitate communication among team members. Virtual teams can be comprised of persons separated by great distances.

Work Breakdown Structure (WBS)

A deliverable orientated hierarchical decomposition of the work to be executed by the project team to accomplish the project objectives and create the required deliverables. It organizes and defines the total scope of the project.

Work Package

A deliverable or project work component at the lowest level of each branch of the work breakdown structure.

Workaround Technique

A response to a negative risk that has occurred. Distinguished from contingency plan in that a workaround is not planned in advance of the occurrence of the risk event.

English/Spanish Glossary

English	Spanish
angle	**angulo** (ahn-goo-loe)
area	**area** (ah-reh-ah)
basement	**sotano** (so-tah-noe)
bathroom	**bano** (bahn-nyoe)
bathtub	**tina** (tee-nah)
bedroom	**recamara** (reh-cam-ah-rah)
brick	**ladrillo** (lah-dree-yoe)
bring	**llevar** (yeh-bar)
cabinet	**armario** (ahr-mah-ree-yoe)
carpenter	**carpintero** (car-peen-tehr-oe)
caulk	**masilla de calafatear** (mah-see-yah deh cah-lah-fah-the-ar)
ceiling	**cielo rao** (see-eh-loe rah-soe)
cement	**hormigon** (hor-mee-gone)
center	**centro** (cen-troe)
connect	**conectar** (coe-neck-tar)
corner	**esquina** (es-skee-nah)
counter	**encimera** (en-see-mahr-ah)
cover	**cubrir** (coo-breer)
cut	**cortar** (cor-tar)
deck	**terraza** (tehr-rah-sah)
dig	**cavar** (cah-var)
dining room	**excavacion** (eks-cah-vah-see-own)
disconnect	**comedor** (coe-meh-door)
door	**desconectar** (des-con-ek-tar)
drain	**drenaje** (dren-ah-hay)
driveway	**camino de entrada** (cah-mee-noe deh en-trah-dah)
drywall	**table-roca** (tah-blah-roe-cah)
electricity	**electrcidad** (ee-lek-trees-ee-dahd)
exterior	**exterior** (eks-tehr-eeror)
fan	**ventilador** (behn-tee-lah-door)
faucet	**llave** (yah-beh)
feet (measurement)	**pie** (pee-yehs)
form	**formar** (for-mar)
foundation	**cimiento** (see-mee-en-toe)
frame	**armazon** (ar-mah-sone-ad-oe)
framing	**armazonado** (ar-mah-sone-ad-oe)
garage	**cochera** (koe-chehr-ah)

TO ORDER CALL: 1-888-356-8085 or henryevansdesign.com   Builder's Advantage: Home Plans Volume 1

English	Spanish
glass	**vidrio** (vee-dree-oe)
glue	**pegar** (peh-gar), **pegamento** (peg-ah-men-toe), **cola** (koe-lah)
gravel	**grava** (grah-bah)
hallway	**pasillo** (pah-see-yoe)
hang	**colocar** (koe-loe-car)
hard hat	**casco** (cahs-coe)
here	**aqui** (ah-key)
house	**casa** (cah-sah)
inches	**pulgadas** (pool-gah-dabs)
insulation	**aislamiento** (ayees-lah-mee-en-toe)
jack (phone)	**enchufe** (en-choo-fay)
jack hammer	**martillo perforador** (mahr-tee-yoe per-for-ah-door)
jamb	**jamba** (jahm-bah)
joint	**juntu** (whoon-tah)
kitchen	**cocina** (koe-see-nah)
ladder	**escalera** (es-kah-lehr-ah)
laundry room	**cuarto de lavar** (kwar-toe deh lah-bar)
level	**nivelar** (nee-veh-lar)
level	**nivel** (nee-vel)
lift	**levanter** (leh-vahn-tar)
living room	**sala** (sah-lah)
lock	**cerradura** (sehr-doo-rah)
long	**largo** (lar-goe)
lumber	**madera** (mah-dehr-ah)
mark	**marcar** (mar-car) **marca** (mar-cah)
measure	**medir** (meh-deer)
mortar	**mortero** (mor-tehr-oe)
nail	**calvo** (klah-voe)
narrow	**angosto** (ahn-goes-toe)
need	**necesitar** (nes-es-eet-ahr), **necesidad** (nes-es-ee-dahd)
new	**nuevo** (new-ay-voe)
open	**abrir** (a-breer)
paint	**pintar** (peen-tar), **pintura** (peen-tor-ah)
paint brush	**brocha** (broe-chah)
painter	**pintor** (peen-tor)
parallel	**paralelo** (pah-rah-le-loe)
patio	**patio** (pah-tee-oe)
pavement	**pavimento** (pah-bee-men-toe)

English	Spanish
pipe	**tubo** (too-boe)
plans	**planes** (plahn-ehs)
plaster	**yeso** (yeh-soe)
plastic	**plastic** (plah-stee-coe)
please	**por favor** (poor-fah-voor)
plumber	**fontanero** (fon-tahn-ehr-oe)
plumbing	**fontaneria** (fon-tahn-eh-ree-ah)
plywood	**madera contrachapada** (mah-dehr-ah con-trah-chah-pah-dah)
post	**poste** (poe-steh)
putty	**masilla** (mah-see-yah)
rafter	**cabrio** (cah-bree-yoe)
retaining wall	**muro de contencion** (mur-oe-deh con-ten-see-ohn)
roof	**techo** (teh-choe)
room	**cuarto** (kwar-toe)
sand	**lijar** (lee-har), **lija** (lee-hah)
sandpaper	**papel de lija** (pah-pell deh lee-hah)
saw	**aserrar** (ah-seer-rah), **sierra** (see-her-rah)
scaffold	**andamio** (an-dahm-ee-oe)
screen	**tela metalica** (teh-lah met-ahl-ee-cah)
screw	**antornillar** (a-tor-nee-yahr), **tornillo** (tor-nee-oe)
sewer	**alcantarilla** (ahl-kahn-tar-ree-yah)
shut	**cerrar** (sehr-rar)
slab	**losa** (loe-sae)
splice	**empalmar** (em-pahl-mar), **empalme** (em-pahl-meh)
square	**escuadrar** (es-kwa-drahr)
stake	**estacar** (es-tah-car), **estaca** (es-tah-cah)
stairs	**escaleras** (es-kah-lehr-ahs)
staple	**grapar** (grah-par)
steel	**acero** (ah-sehr-oe)
straight	**recto** (rek-toe)
stucco	**estuco** (es-took-oe)
tape measure	**cinta metrica** (seen-tah meh-tree-cah)
tar	**brea** (breh-ah)
telephone	**telephono** (tel-ef-oe-noe)
that's all	**eso es todo** (es-oe es toe-doe)
tile	**azulejo** (ah-soo-leh-hoe)
time	**tiempo** (tee-em-poe)

English	Spanish
tools	**herramientas** (eir-ah-mee-en-tahs)
trash	**basura** (bah-soor-ah)
trim	**acabar, terminar** (ah-kah-bar, ter-mee-nar)
truck	**camion** (kah-mee-ohn)
under	**bajo** (bah-hoe)
underground	**subterraneo** (soob-tehr-rahn-neh-oe)
understand	**comprender** (comb-pren-dare)
unload	**descargar** (des-cahr-gahr)
up, above	**arriba** (ah-ree-bah)
wall	**muro, pared** (mur-oe), (pah-red)
wash	**lavar** (lah-bar)
watch out!	**Cuidado** (kwee-dahd-oe)
water	**regar** (reh-gar) **agua** (ah-gwah)
wheel barrow	**carretilla** (car-reh-tee-yah)
when	**cuando** (kwahn-doe)
where	**donde** (don-day)
who	**quien** (kee-en)
how	**como** (coe-moe)
why	**por que** (por-kay)
window	**ventana** (ven-tahn-ah)
wire	**alambre** (a-lahm-breh)
work	**trabajo** (trah-bah-hoe)
worker	**trabajador** (tra-bah-hah-dor)
wrench	**llave de tuercas** (yah-beh deh twer-kahs)

Useful English/Spanish Expressions

English	Spanish
What is your name?	**Como se llama?** (koe-moe say yahm-ah)
Thank you.	**Gracias.** (grahs-ee-ahs)
You are welcome.	**De nada.** (deh nah-dah)
Start the job _ (today, tomorrow).	**Comience el trabajo ___ (hoy, manana).** (coe-mee-ens-eh el-trah-bah-hoe oy mahn-yahn-ah)
The job pays _ (an hour, day, per job).	**Por este trabajo se paga _ (por hora, por dia o por trabajo).** (poor es-teh trah-bah-hoe seh paa-gaa) _ (poor or-ah poor dee-ah, poor tra-bah-hoe)
How many?	**Cuantos?** (kwahn-toes)
How much?	**Cuanto?** (kwahn-toe)
How much do you need?	**Cuanto necesita?** (kwahn-toe nes-es-eet-ah)
I will pay you on _ .	**Le pagare el _ .** (leh pah-gah-ray el)
Monday.	**Lunes.** (loo-nehs)
Tuesday.	**Martes.** (mar-tehs)
Wednesday.	**Miercoles.** (mee-ehr-coe-lehs)
Thursday.	**Jueves.** (whey-vehs)
Friday.	**Viernes.** (vee-ehr-nehs)
Saturday.	**Sabado.** (sah-bah-doe)
Sunday.	**Domingo.** (doe-ming-oe)
Well done.	**Buen trabajo.** (bwein trah-bah-hoe)